POWER OVER POTS

A family guide
for managing
POSTURAL
ORTHOSTATIC
TACHYCARDIA
SYNDROME

SCHELDON KRESS, M.D.

Scheldon Kress, M.D. is currently employed as a Medical Officer in the Division of Medical Imaging Products at the Food and Drug Administration in Silver Spring, Maryland. **POWER over POTS – A Family Guide for Managing POTS** reflects the views of the author and should not be construed to represent FDA's views and policies.

Scheldon Kress, M.D. is a specialist in Internal Medicine with over 30 years of clinical experience caring for patients with challenging medical problems. He is passionate about helping patients and pioneered educational and behavioral management programs for many medical conditions while in practice in Northern Virginia.

Medical Disclaimer

The information provided is not intended to substitute for the advice of a personal physician. The material provided is for educational purposes only, designed to help patients and their families become more knowledgeable about diagnosing and treating POTS. **POWER over POTS** will help POTS patients and their families seek out medical specialists who can manage individuals with this mysterious illness. Most practicing physicians are unfamiliar with the existence of POTS and when asked - admit that they have never seen a case. **POWER over POTS** can help you find physicians who specialize in the rehabilitation of patients with POTS.

Medical information is an ever-changing science. Knowledge regarding POTS will continue to proliferate based on ever-expanding research and clinical experience. In fact, many investigators are currently seeking clues as to why only some adolescents acquire POTS. Every effort has been made by the author to present accurate information as available at the time of publishing. However, the author cannot be responsible for expected evolving new knowledge in this fast-moving field.

Likewise, the links provided were operable as of December 2016. Whereas investigators frequently move from one medical facility to another, it may be difficult to track them down.

Table of Contents

List of Tables

List of Figures

List of Recovery Records

ACKNOWLEDGEMENTS

To my loving family and friends for their support while working on my book.

My family inspires me to continue learning while also educating others. Their love, participation and support have enabled this book to become a reality. A special thank you to my wonderful wife, Rose, for her unconditional love and support. My gratitude to my loving children and their spouses: Michael & Mimi, Karen & Ira and Julie & Marc. Much love to all of my grandchildren who bring me tremendous joy: Max, Sam, Adam, Justin, Jenna, Jason and Brandon. Adam's journey to a correct diagnosis of POTS and strategies to overcoming POTS provided the inspiration for me to learn about POTS. His parents, Karen and Ira, shared their experiences with having a teenager managing the symptoms of, and implementing the strategies for recovery in **POWER over POTS**.

To the many professionals that supported my book process:

Jonathan Dimes (JDimes MedVisual Communications) for your educational illustrations that were able to turn complex subject matter into easily understood graphic images.

Michael Bennett Kress (MBK Photography) for your talent and artistic direction for my photo.

Karen Hammerman, Sc.M. for the many hours of support and dedication in helping me complete my book.

Julie Schumacher (sasse agency) for her leadership and development of the **POWER over POTS** brand. A special thank you to your team including Reid Stiegman for his insight and expertise in turning an enlightening message into an inspiring cover image. You both captured not only the blueness experienced by those with POTS, but also added multiple points of light (knowledge) that can lead to **POWER over POTS**.

To the medical community and patients:

Thank you to the many medical professionals that collaborated with me to ensure that the most updated and accurate information was included in my book. Also, I would like to thank the Cardiologists, Internists, advocates and those struggling with POTS who read my book and provided feedback including *reviews* to share.

INTRODUCTION

While POTS is among one of the most common medical disorders affecting adolescents and young adults, both health care professionals and patients generally know very little about this condition. The majority of POTS (postural orthostatic tachycardia syndrome) patients suffer with mysterious and frightening symptoms while searching for a diagnosis. And without a proper diagnosis, there is no possibility of treatment. Otherwise healthy appearing adolescents, primarily females, frequently report racing hearts, headaches, fatigue, weakness, dizziness, "brain fog," visual and abdominal disturbances. Such symptoms play havoc on one's lifestyle by curtailing one's daily activities.

During the past 15 years, many medical centers have studied POTS patients and have determined the mechanisms responsible for this bizarre condition. The body's difficulty adjusting to the upright position has been proven to be due to gravitational shifting of blood to the lower body while upright which results in decreased heart outflow. This consumer health book is for both patients and family members. It explains in simplified terms the scientific mechanisms responsible for POTS, how to correct the malfunctioning mechanisms and provides a step-by-step program for beating POTS. If you or a loved one has POTS, this book is for you. Every page is packed with facts you need to know. You will find this **POTS Recovery Program** enlightening and beneficial.

Like so many physicians, I knew nothing about POTS, and went through three agonizing years until we found the cause of my grandson's scary illness - POTS. Many medical specialists were unable to explain his head-aches, fatigue, "tunnel vision" and especially, his short-term memory loss. This bright 16 year old was suddenly unable to participate in his classes, complete his schoolwork and enjoy social activities with his friends. Yet, once he found knowledgeable POTS specialists, he was able to navigate POTS, take back his life, become his college mascot, graduate from college and even climb 14,000 foot mountain peaks with friends.

A general lack of knowledge about the mechanisms responsible for POTS and its treatment stimulated me to review the published medical literature dealing with POTS. Hundreds of articles have been published in medical journals dealing with POTS over the past 25 years. It's not clear why the world-wide medical literature is so rich with information, yet that infor-mation is not well disseminated to physicians. Most physicians have no knowledge of this condition. Thus, physicians do not consider the pos-sibility that POTS might be the cause for the puzzling symptoms of the patient being examined. POTS has been called a "missed and misdiag-nosed disorder."

Most alterations in body physiology responsible for the reduced return of blood from the lower body to the heart and brain are correctable. You may be asking: "What is POTS? What causes POTS? Why did I get POTS? How do I get better? How long will it take to get well? Will I be able to return to school full-time? Will I be able to play sports again? Will I ever lead a nor-mal life again?" You may be asking a lot of similar questions. **POWER over POTS** helps provide answers to these and many other questions.

Writing this book is my attempt to "spread-the-word" and explain the causes and treatments in an easy-to-understand manner. No longer is it necessary for adolescents and young adults to suffer with the life-disrupt-ing symptoms of POTS. This **POWER over POTS** Recovery Program provides knowledge. Knowledge is power that can help you to understand

POTS, seek out knowledgeable POTS specialists and successfully navigate POTS and recover.

While written for patients with this debilitating illness and their families, many health care professionals can find this information and the therapeutic plan, the **POWER over POTS** Recovery Program, useful in the management of their POTS patients. Most POTS patients will eventually be free of symptoms. For those with the most severe symptoms, recovery may take longer. Some may need referral to a major POTS center where recognized authoritative resources provide help.

Steps to begin the healing process are not possible until a diagnosis is confirmed. Enabling you to shorten the delay in establishing a diagnosis and initiate early and successful treatment are the primary goals of this book. Hopefully, with this book in hand, you can gain the necessary knowledge to manage your illness, take back your life and attain **POWER over POTS**.

CHAPTER 1:

What is POTS?

Why Is It Called POTS?

Postural Orthostatic Tachycardia Syndrome (POTS) may sound like a mouthful, but when broken down, it refers to a common medical condition that is rarely recognized even by well-trained and experienced physicians. Postural (relates to posture), orthostatic (relates to being upright), tachycardia (relates to rapid heart rate) and syndrome (relates to a collection of symptoms). POTS is not a disease. POTS is a recognized chronic medical condition identified with increasing frequency among otherwise healthy appearing adolescents and young adults. Like so many others, you must have lots of questions you want to ask. Let's get started, this book has the answers you're looking for.

It has been estimated that as many as 3 million young Americans share the symptoms of this bizarre condition. More are discovered daily. POTS has even been recognized world-wide. It has been recognized primarily among children, teenagers and young adults. Most cases go unrecognized and undiagnosed. Even though symptoms most frequently start around adolescence, they can be present for decades before the diagnosis is recognized. Currently almost fifty articles appear in medical journals each year reporting on studies of POTS by medical investigators from around the world. While the sudden appearance of so many articles dealing with POTS suggests a worldwide epidemic - actually all it confirms is growing recognition and interest in this disorder.

POTS is characterized by rapid heartbeat when standing upright. The primary symptom complex consists of orthostatic (standing upright) intolerance - the body's difficulty adjusting to the upright position. Rapid heart rate occurs upon assuming an upright posture or standing position and slowly reverses when sitting or reclining. When considering the presence of POTS, dehydration, medications and many debilitating diseases need to be excluded, as their symptoms can mimic POTS.

All symptoms of POTS are related to an excessive gravitational shifting of blood from the upper to the lower body - decreased refilling of the heart - decreased cardiac output - and sympathetic nervous system over-activity. Among the most common symptoms are fatigue, headaches, light-headedness, "brain fog," eye and abdominal disturbances. Symptoms may be constant or vary from day to day or week to week, but need to be present for at least 3-6 months to establish the diagnosis.

POTS is best recognized by the absolute heart rate rising by greater than 30 beats per minute (BPM) or exceeding 120 BPM without a fall in blood pressure within 8 to 10 minutes of going from the supine (lying flat) position to an orthostatic (upright or head-up) posture in the absence of another chronic disorder. Typically, the rise in heart rate occurs within the first 2 minutes of assuming an upright position. Among children and teens the absolute heart rate rises by greater than 40 beats per minute (BPM) and may exceed 130 BPM, more than among young adults. While fatigue, lightheadedness and feeling faint are common components, low blood pressure (hypotension) is not a common finding characteristic of POTS.

Lack of the presence of a known single cause does not diminish the severe physical, mental and social incapacitation experienced by those who have POTS and the strain on their families.

How Common Is POTS?

Imagine a high achieving middle school student, who suddenly has severe headaches most mornings, cannot recall homework assignments or significant recent events. Imagine a teenager who gets exhausted after minimal activity. Imagine a teenager who declines to participate in favorite activities such as parties with friends, shopping or attending a favorite team's sporting event. Imagine athletes who are suddenly too fatigued to get out of bed and forced to restrict their activities. POTS can be this debilitating! It's estimated that as many as 3 million Americans suffer with POTS, with millions more worldwide. The incidence is estimated at up to 170/100,000, primarily female Caucasians. The highest incidence is among teens, twenty and thirty year olds. Most frequently the initial symptoms start around adolescence, with peak onset between 10 and 19 years of age. Many POTS patients are aware of a family member who recalls having similar POTS-like symptoms when they were younger.

When Did POTS Start?

When Homo sapiens (earliest man) first assumed an upright posture, the circulatory system was presented with a new physiological challenge. The circulatory system had to figure out how to move blood from the legs "upward against gravity," all the way up to that all-important brain. When the body is upright, both during standing and walking, the circulatory system is most stressed. How can the body move blood up the legs against gravity? Returning blood from the legs back to the heart is a challenge even among normal individuals. Rather than having diseased organs, POTS represents autonomic dysfunction (failure of several automatic bodily functions). Automatic processes are responsible for maintaining upward circulation while upright. Normal complex biologic processes (automatic bodily functions) are responsible for ensuring return of blood from the lower body to critical organs like the heart and brain.

What the upright body requires is a reliable autonomic nervous system – a survival system able to immediately respond to this relative volume shift - step-in and set in process mechanisms to increase heart rate, tension of the leg blood vessels and cardiac output to protect brain blood flow.

POTS can be compared to an adolescent with a newly acquired skyscraper body (tall structure) that has grown quickly – but, the building's electrical wiring system (autonomic functions) has not yet matured fully and is malfunctioning. Rapid growth spurts test the ability of an immature autonomic (automatic bodily functions) system to cope with a rapidly enlarging physical structure

---

Why POTS Picks On Teenagers?

Most frequently the onset of POTS symptoms coincides with the puberty growth spurt of adolescence. Adolescence is an important period of developmental change. Puberty is associated with maturing of many biological systems including sexual, brain and nervous systems. **POTS can be compared to an adolescent with a newly acquired skyscraper body (tall structure) that has grown quickly – but, the building's electrical wiring system (autonomic functions) has not yet matured fully and is malfunctioning. Rapid growth spurts test the ability of an immature autonomic (automatic bodily functions) system to cope with a rapidly**

enlarging physical structure. The autonomic processes, by necessity, must keep making adjustments to keep up with the latest skyscraper growth. What worked well last year must adjust further for today's taller body. Peak incidence of POTS occurs in the 10-30 year age group.

While the onset of POTS usually peaks at puberty, symptoms may only be present for a short term, last for a few years or persist for many decades. Of great importance in distinguishing POTS from other disorders, the symptoms of POTS did not exist during childhood.

Complex physiological processes (automatic bodily functions) - cardiovascular, neurological and muscular are required to perform efficiently and in harmony to correct the excessive pooling of blood to the lower body and maintain normal return of blood to the heart when upright. As the body grows taller, the task becomes more complex.

Why Does It Take So Long To Get Diagnosed With POTS?

While POTS cases are diagnosed daily, most patients go unrecognized and undiagnosed - suffering for years or decades before being diagnosed. When POTS patients initially seek help, they present with a laundry list of symptoms and no observable abnormal physical findings. They complain of symptoms like headaches, fatigue, being lightheaded, confused at times, rapid heartbeats, blurry vision and possibly abdominal pain. And, even after an extensive physical examination and routine screening laboratory testing - nothing abnormal is found. Therefore, most frequently they get pegged as being psychologically stressed out and they leave the doctor's office without a diagnosis and without treatment. Most often they are told, "There's nothing wrong with you. It's all in your head!" Many are referred to additional specialists and even psychiatrists. Again, without useful answers.

POTS is a relatively new medical condition. Unfortunately, the majority of physicians in America know nothing about this puzzling condition known as POTS including: what is it, what causes it, how to treat it, and how to help patients recover! With time, the ability to function while standing becomes limited, fatigue worsens and these youngsters spend greater portions of the day in bed. Now, school, work and social activities become disrupted. Then even friends and relatives begin to suspect that these young POTS patients are "faking it" to get attention.

On average, POTS patients consult with 2 to 7 physicians before the diagnosis of POTS is even suspected. According to Dysautonomia International, on average POTS patients struggle with this frustrating and debilitating illness for almost 6 years before obtaining a diagnosis.

> *Adam,* age 16, presented with a complex diagnostic picture. He suffered with headaches, blurred vision, exhaustion and severe short-term memory loss for 15 months. He had been evaluated by no less than 6 specialists, a pediatrician, diagnostician, neurologists and cardiologists and none had determined the cause of his symptoms. Each specialist ordered more tests, but none provided useful information. Instead of a Tilt Table Test, Adam had many specialized tests including brain waves, middle ear testing and brain magnetic resonance imaging (MRI).*
>
> *To add to the family's frustration, while Adam was having a spinal tap performed, the nurse said to the mother, "Why are you subjecting Adam to all these unnecessary painful tests when there is nothing wrong with him?" Eventually Adam was evaluated by a POTS specialist who made the correct diagnosis and initiated a program that gave him back his life. In Adam's case, his mother's persistence and*

ignoring the professional negativity while seeking help for her incapacitated son, gave him the opportunity to recover.

When discussing his illness with friends at school, Adam told them, "POTS sucks!!" He told his friends," I hope no one else has to go through such a terrible ordeal as I did, to get treated."

*(Illustrative cases are simulated, but are representative of real-life POTS experiences.)

Believing the Symptoms or Not?

Health care providers see a wide assortment of patients and need to sort out which illness the patient may have and what's the optimum approach to their management. Being a health care provider caring for a patient with difficult to explain symptoms can be among the most challenging of tasks for responsible health care providers.

Health care providers are often puzzled by the bizarre collections of symptoms like those presented by POTS patients. They may question whether the symptoms are real or not. They may suspect that either the adolescent or their parent or both are utilizing sickness to get out of school or work. Such individuals may even be suspected of fabricating symptoms because they crave medical attention and sympathy. People have been known to fake illnesses for a variety of reasons.

There are even patients that see health care providers who are "hypochondriacs." They actually worry excessively about horrible symptoms and sicknesses they don't have. Others have a factitious disorder known as "Munchausen syndrome." Munchausen patients know they are not sick, but go from one healthcare provider to the next, telling fake stories about their illnesses and seeking unnecessary treatment strictly for attention. Mothers with Munchausen by Proxy Syndrome have been known to take pride in being such a devoted mother while caring for such children, all the while exposing the child to unnecessary risky procedures and surgery. Whereas it's estimated that 1,000 cases of Munchausen by Proxy Syndrome related child abuse are seen annually, health care providers do need to be on the alert for such occurrences of malingering. However, health care providers need to thoroughly evaluate each puzzling case, before labeling a difficult to explain case as a hypochondriac or "Munchausen syndrome" patient.

Over a 6 month period of time, Donna, age 16, was evaluated by an ophthalmologist (eye doctor), neuro-ophthalmologist (brain-eye specialist), ENT (ear nose & throat), infectious disease specialist, 4 cardiologists (heart specialist) and 4 neurologists (nervous system specialists). She was seeking help for her headaches, blurred vision, lightheadedness, dizziness, lack of energy and trouble recalling events. She had had similar, but milder, symptoms when she was 13, but evaluations done at that time had failed to reveal a cause. But, after a recent virus, the symptoms had returned and increased in intensity.

One neurologist recommended to Donna's parents, "Dial down your dialogue with her. If you stop talking to her about her symptoms, she'll stop paying attention to them!" Another neurologist recommended psychiatric counselling. Following that psychiatric consultation, she couldn't even remember meeting with the psychiatrist. One neurologist's assistant castigated Donna's mother for insisting on more tests. She told Donna's mother, "You keep insisting on tests for your daughter, but they are always normal. There is nothing wrong with your daughter! Have you ever considered that the problem is YOU?"

Her extensive testing included:

- Countless blood tests

- Several eye examinations

- Doppler studies of major neck arteries

- Somatosensory Potential (small nerve function)

- Ambulatory electroencephalogram (brain waves)

- Electrocardiogram

- ENG – Electronystagmography (brain and eye)

- ECOG – Electrocochleogram (brain and middle ear)

- Spinal tap (examination of spinal fluid)

- MRI (magnetic resonance imaging) of brain and neck

- MRA (magnetic resonance angiography) of major blood vessels of brain and neck

None of these many tests were abnormal. In fact, none would be expected to be abnormal in a POTS patient. They were performed to rule out other serious medical conditions that could produce similar symptoms, but they never helped make a diagnosis of POTS. It took 3 long years from the onset of symptoms at the age of 13, till the confirmation of Donna's diagnosis of POTS at age 16. When finally evaluated by a cardiologist specializing in POTS, several specialized diagnostic tests for POTS (not readily available) confirmed the diagnosis of POTS. Her Tilt Table Test was abnormal – pulse rose from 66 to 120 beats per minute when tilted - a rise of 54 beats (more than 40 beats per minute). An Impedance Cardiogram test determined that her stroke volume (blood pumped per beat) and cardiac output (blood pumped per minute) fell significantly when tilted, confirming a significant drop-off in heart output when upright.

As demonstrated, evaluating young adults with undiagnosed POTS is always challenging for both parents and health care providers. As a POTS patient, you need to be assertive, explaining your symptoms as accurately as possible including details regarding:

Onset of symptoms (age, year, time of day and season)

- Frequency of symptoms (times per day, per week and per month)
- Severity (quantify level of energy, fatigue, weakness and incapacitation)
- Influence of body position (standing, sitting, reclining and exercising)
- Onset following a viral-like illness with fever
- Influence of meals, hydration, activities, room temperature and menses
- Disturbance of thinking ("foggy thinking," difficulty focusing and memory loss)
- Disturbance of vision (blurring, restricted and diminished)
- Disturbance of sleep (unrefreshing sleep, daytime sleepiness and restless sleep)
- Factors that improve or aggravate your condition

Give your health care provider as many clues as you can. The more clues you can provide, the easier it will be for your health care provider to recognize that the symptoms are real and the source of your problem, might just be POTS. (See **Chapter 7 - What Are the Clues to Diagnosis of POTS**)

During orthostatic stress (standing upright) in individuals with POTS, there is exaggerated gravitational pooling of blood downward. A greater collection of blood shifts from the chest towards the lower abdomen, thighs and legs compared to people without POTS.

What Is The Role Of Gravity?

During orthostatic stress (standing upright) in individuals with POTS, there is exaggerated gravitational pooling of blood downward. A greater collection of blood shifts from the chest towards the lower abdomen, thighs and legs compared to people without POTS. When standing, it's estimated that 25% of the central body blood gravitates from the chest towards the lower abdomen, thighs and legs. Because there is reduced return of blood to the heart when upright, there is a reduced volume of blood pumped with each subsequent heartbeat. The quantity of blood pumped out with each heartbeat is known as the *stroke volume*. Specifically, during standing in individuals with POTS, the cardiac output (quantity of blood pumped out per minute) is substantially reduced. The more severe the reduction in *cardiac output* and brain blood flow - the greater the reduction in nourishment of the brain and severity of symptoms.

What Is The Role Of Muscular Deconditioning?

Most adolescents who have not participated in regular strenuous exercise for a prolonged period of time develop weakened body muscles (the "use it or lose it" rule). This deconditioning takes place in the skeletal muscles and even the heart muscle. Sitting all day in classes and at the computer encourages the "use it or lose it" process. The deconditioning seen in POTS patients is similar to that seen after prolonged inactivity in bed or space flight. Lack of regular exercise and inactivity can be associated with heart deconditioning, atrophy of heart muscle (loss of muscle due to reduced use) with a resultant smaller sized weaker heart. Atrophy of the heart muscle often seen in individuals with POTS further contributes to a reduced cardiac output. Today's adolescents spend too much sedentary time on computers, cell phones, watching television, doing homework and sitting in classes. Therefore, they are more prone to deconditioning or weakening of both their heart and leg muscles.

What Is The Role Of Reduced Blood Volume?

Blood volume is maintained by adequate intake of liquids and salt. Many young people have low blood volume due to low intake of fluids and salt. Often they also are found to have reduced renin (body's salt retaining hormone). Reduced circulating blood volume within the vascular system further diminishes blood flow - in general, to and from the heart.

What Is the Role Of Nerves To The Veins?

Veins are the thin tubes that lead back to and carry blood back to the heart. Most veins of the arms, thighs and legs contain valves. These valves are small door-like structures that only open in one direction and prevent blood from going backwards. Walls of veins contain a muscular layer that can respond to nervous signals. Sympathetic nerves stimulate these muscles causing constriction (squeezing) of the veins and parasympathetic nerves stimulate dilatation (relaxation) of the veins. Constriction speeds up return of blood to the heart and dilatation discourages return and encourages pooling.

Among some POTS patients, the veins of the lower body exhibit a dysautonomic response (malfunction). Specifically, they are unable to respond and contract to sympathetic stimulation. These vein walls ignore the message to constrict and to speed-up venous blood flow back to the heart. Instead, the veins stay relaxed. Why the veins fail to respond to the signal to constrict remains unclear. Is it nervous tissue immaturity or injury?

Is POTS Associated With Preceding Infections?

In many cases the onset of POTS symptoms may follow an acute illness with fever, headache, fatigue, weight loss, joint or generalized achiness. Symptoms can also arise after a prolonged period of inactivity that follows a major injury or surgery. In fact, the symptoms of POTS are frequently attributed to that preceding event. Therefore, infectious diseases like influenza, Lyme disease, infectious mononucleosis, Epstein B and other viral infections or even encephalitis (brain infections) are suspected as possibly being responsible for the unexplained symptoms. To everyone's disappointment, usually the test results for these infectious and brain disorders do not provide useful information. If positive, the test results more often imply history of a prior infection. Even if the infection is only coincidental, it may actually play a role in triggering or worsening of the POTS symptoms. Just like the "straw that broke the camel's back" – POTS was already present, but the illness or injury acted like a trigger initiating the worsening of symptoms and awareness of its presence.

> *Justin aged 15, developed a viral-like illness with fever and general achiness for a week. During the next 12 weeks he developed increasing fatigue, headaches, memory impairment, blurred vision, rapid heart and joint pains. His symptoms all seemed to become worse when he first got out of bed in the morning. Initial evaluation by his pediatrician suspected Lyme disease. He was treated with doxycycline for 4 weeks for possible Lyme disease. When he did not show any evidence of improvement, his neurologist requested a spinal fluid examination which was normal. A year later he had a Tilt Table Test that confirmed his diagnosis of POTS.*

In retrospect, his viral illness did not cause his POTS illness. However, it may have intensified his inability to overcome his hidden orthostatic intolerance (symptoms brought-on-by-standing) making his POTS symptoms more obvious and recognizable.

What is the Role of the Immune System?

The immune system is essential for life; it normally helps the body fight off infections by producing antibodies that destroy invading organisms. Sometime these foreign organisms share common components with our own body tissues. When this occurs, the antibodies also become auto-antibodies (antibodies against one's own tissues). Auto-antibodies are capable of attacking the body's own cells and tissues resulting in an auto-immune-disease (disease caused by antibodies against self). Examples of auto-immune diseases caused by auto-antibodies include diabetes mellitus (pancreas), multiple sclerosis (brain and spinal cord), inflammatory bowel disease (small intestine), rheumatoid arthritis (joints) and thyroiditis (thyroid gland).

Antibodies to veins and nervous tissues have been observed among small numbers of patients with POTS. The significance of these findings has not been fully explained. One possible explanation is that these antibodies can attack and block the sympathetic nervous system signal (epinephrine) to the lower body veins to tighten and encourage movement of blood upward.

Why Does POTS Pick On Girls?

POTS occurs predominantly among females. Approximately 80% of POTS cases are found in females. Females can experience POTS symptoms throughout their childbearing years (13 to 50). Most commonly the onset of symptoms of POTS among young females begins following the onset of menstruation, early during a first pregnancy or in the course of another illness. Whereas symptoms worsen during menses and early in pregnancies, symptoms are often wrongly attributed to menstruation or to pregnancy only - in both cases masking the actual diagnosis.

Why the incidence of POTS is greater among teen girls is still a mystery. While it's known that females exhibit major fluctuations in sex hormones during the menstrual cycle, those changes alone don't explain the disorder. We do know that orthostatic intolerance tends to be more severe immediately after a menstrual period when female hormones and blood volume are at their lowest levels. At the same time, stroke volume and cardiac output fall the most during standing. Post ovulation (post mid-cycle) when both estrogen and progesterone levels rise, renin is activated to promote salt and water retention by the kidneys.

Females start out with smaller sized hearts than males. Thus, their hearts pump out a lower volume of blood with each heartbeat. Add deconditioning of the heart and muscles due to inactivity to their already reduced blood volume, and females attain the perfect set-up for POTS.

Why Is My Heart Racing?

POTS is characterized by a fast pounding heart when standing upright. The primary symptom complex consists of orthostatic (standing upright) intolerance, the body's difficulty adjusting to the upright position. The rapid heart rate occurs upon assuming an upright posture or standing position and slowly reverses when sitting or reclining.

Tachycardia (rapid heartbeat) during an orthostatic challenge, a key component of POTS, is among the most frequent symptoms experienced by those with this disorder. Tachycardia may be associated with palpitations. Palpitations describe the feeling that one's heart is racing, pounding, beating irregularly or skipping beats. The tachycardia is caused by turning on the sympathetic nervous system into overdrive, our body's attempt to restore blood flow to the brain. With the reduction in blood returning to the heart caused by standing, a fast beating heart becomes the body's initial attempt to overcome the reduced cardiac outflow. The tachycardia of POTS may often be associated with anxiety, shortness of breath and even panic attacks. Anxiety and panic states frequently lead to rapid shallow chest breathing (hyperventilation). Chest pain frequently accompanies hyperventilation due to the over stretching of the joints of the rib-cage.

Why Do I Have Lightheadedness and Headaches?

Most POTS patients have reduced brain perfusion (decreased blood flow) and experience lightheadedness and headaches. The majority of POTS patients report having headaches and headaches can take on a variety of forms. Headaches may be localized, for example behind the eyes or back of the head. Or, headaches can take on a migraine pattern with associated nausea, vomiting and vertigo (dizziness). Headaches most often occur during standing (orthostatic headaches) and are frequently preceded by or associated with lightheadedness or dizziness.

For most, the headaches and associated symptoms are more severe early in the day, for others they are worse as the day progresses. Headaches can be made worse following coughing, straining for bowel movements and leaning the head forward. For some, the headaches occur daily, for others they occur irregularly. Lying down or going back to bed generally relieves most POTS - related headaches.

Others complain additionally of light headedness, attention difficulties, or nausea when upright. Patients with more severe symptoms of orthostatic intolerance also complain of weakness, dizziness, drowsiness, visual disturbances, diminished concentration, chest or abdominal pain, rapid heart rate or shortness of breath. Most patients have their own unique grouping of symptoms that keep recurring.

Some of the symptoms associated with brain hypoperfusion (decreased brain blood flow) have taken on distinctive characteristics resulting in unique descriptive names. A unique headache seen with brain hypoperfusion of POTS is the "coat-hanger headache" pattern (pain back of head, neck and shoulders).

In addition to trouble concentrating and memory loss, Jason, age 22, suffered with headaches (pain behind eyes, back of head and shoulders) which tended to be worse in the morning when arising. When in elevators and on airplanes, he felt tremendous pressure and pain in his head, so severe at times he was unable to speak.

Over the next 15 months, he continued to experience dizziness, flushing of his face, and severe daily headaches immediately upon standing up and getting out of bed in the morning. In the summer, as the temperature increased, his symptoms became more severe and he became desperate for help. Finally, a neurologist raised the possibility of POTS, and a Tilt Table Test confirmed the POTS diagnosis.

The more the blood flow to the brain is compromised, the more severe are the resultant "brain-fog-related" POTS symptoms. Most often among POTS patients, symptoms become more severe the longer one is upright and tend to only improve when lying down.

What Is "Brain Fog?"

Cognition - thinking, learning and remembering are the responsibilities of the brain. The brain is the most complex body organ and is most vulnerable to decreased blood flow and oxygenation. In fact, many of the most disturbing symptoms associated with severe POTS are a result of insufficient blood flow to the brain with compromised oxygen and essential nutrients. The brain's 200 billion nerve cells are interconnected and all depend on a continuous supply of nourishment to perform their many complex functions. Critical higher level processing centers of the brain depend on this continuous supply of oxygenated blood. Without a rich supply of oxygenated blood, a person's attention, sight, problem solving ability and memory suffer. The more the blood flow to the brain is compromised, the more severe are the resultant "brain-fog-related" POTS symptoms. Most often among POTS patients, symptoms become more severe the longer one is upright and tend to only improve when lying down.

In general, those patients who experience "brain fog" symptoms due to hypoperfusion (diminished blood flow) experience dizziness, lightheadedness, difficulty focusing, forgetfulness and both short-term and long-term memory loss. Other investigators have described the "brain fog" as mental clouding, altered executive functioning, impaired cognitive processing and difficulty concentrating and multitasking. Syncope (passing out) and near-syncope (feeling faint) are also common.

"Brain fog" is not limited to POTS. Brain fog also occurs in patients with Alzheimer's disease, mast cell disorders, autism spectrum disorders, chronic fatigue syndrome, Ehlers-Danlos syndrome, drugs and neuropsychiatric disorders. Awareness that "brain fog" is an important and common component of POTS is a recent discovery. Just a few years ago, even POTS specialists didn't accept POTS as a cause of impaired intellectual function. Fortunately, the mental clouding among POTS patients is episodic, primarily during and after being upright. Still today, it's not well recognized that the impairment can be so severe as to resemble Alzheimer's disease, but it can. No wonder, these patients endure test after test looking for another explanation for their bizarre unexplained altered brain functioning.

Sam is a 16 year old teenager who gradually developed Alzheimer's-like memory loss. In addition he noted dizziness and blurred vision when standing for a while. His school mates accused him of being "absent minded" all the time. He couldn't remember school assignments. Most disturbing and incapacitating was this forgetfulness of events of the day prior (hours to whole days). Segments of his days just disappeared, and he was unaware they were missing. He also complained of fatigue, headaches and racing heart. Sam suffered with these mysterious symptoms for 3 years, before learning he had POTS – an immature circulatory system having trouble adjusting to being upright after his growth spurt. He experienced many scary episodes of memory loss like the following:

- Even though he was looking forward to the day that he would get his driving permit, he decided to stop driving lessons because he felt it was unsafe for him to drive.

- He went fishing with his father several times, but could not recall the most recent trip.

- Checking his digital camera, he was shocked to find a beautiful photo of a post-storm sky. He recalled the thunderstorm from the night prior, but didn't remember capturing the post-storm sky photo with his new digital camera.

Alarming symptoms like these with no diagnosis would frighten any teen and their parents. Fearing they were overlooking a serious disease like a brain tumor, his parents took him from medical specialist to medical specialist for several years seeking answers. Eventually, a specialist diagnosed POTS and a recovery program improved most of his symptoms within 9 months.

Why Do I Have Visual Difficulties?

Why do I experience difficulty focusing, blurring and even temporary loss of vision? Reduced blood flow to the brain's visual centers can result in a variety of disturbances of vision. A unique visual disturbance seen with POTS is called tunneling (narrowing of the visual field to resemble looking through a tube), referred to as the "Alice-in-Wonderland" pattern.

Similar to most POTS symptoms, these visual disturbances are primarily associated with the upright position, tend to worsen the longer one is upright and are not permanent.

> *Julie, age 17, experienced headaches, lightheadedness, dizziness and blurring of vision for about 4 months. These tended to be worse while standing. Sometimes her vision would be blurred, or she would have "tunnel vision" (as if looking through a tube) or be blacked-out. Periodically, she felt so exhausted, she felt the necessity to lie down and rest. However, rest rarely improved her headaches, visual difficulties or fatigue.*
>
> *She consulted at least 5 doctors who were unable to find anything medically "wrong." None offered any useful help. Not only was she sick of being sick, but she thought something was really wrong and no one was taking her seriously. Several months later, a friend at school recognized that Julie's symptoms resembled another friend's symptoms who was diagnosed with POTS. Julie made an appointment*

*with that friend's physician, was diagnosed properly and
started on the road to recovery.*

Why Do I Have Abdominal Pain?

Many POTS patients report experiencing abdominal symptoms. The most frequent are nausea, bloating, abdominal cramping and pain. Most often the abdominal symptoms are associated with standing or come on after eating a large meal. When severe, patients tend to spend considerable portions of the day reclining instead of standing and/or avoid eating so as to minimize their abdominal discomfort. Unfortunately, if untreated, as symptoms worsen weight loss follows.

Normally, both during standing and following ingestion of a large meal, the volume of blood within the abdomen increases. When standing, gravity shifts significant quantities of blood from the chest towards the lower body. After eating a large meal, the body likewise shifts significant quantities of blood to the abdominal organs to aid in digestion and absorption of nutrients. POTS patients report having their worst abdominal symptoms associated with both of these activities: standing and after larger meals. Both are associated with reduced circulating blood volume and abdominal symptoms related to diminished blood flow. Why this larger than usual volume of blood results in such severe abdominal symptoms is not clearly understood. However, it is suspected that overstretching of the venous blood vessels, slowing of circulation and alterations to the intestinal nerves are responsible for the symptoms.

*Marc, age 14, experienced unexplained racing heart
and lightheadedness when standing for about 6
months. This was followed by the onset of abdominal pain, nausea and vomiting following many of
his evening meals. Soon afterwards, he noted bloating and nausea after lunch. Before long, he started*

skipping meals to avoid suffering afterwards. Over the next 4 months he missed 24 days of school and lost 15 pounds of weight.

Finally, his doctors solved the mystery, diagnosed his problem and started him on a treatment program. After 3 months of intense lifestyle changes and medication, he was able to eat, attend school every day and his symptoms diminished considerably.

Because of the complexity of the symptomatology of patients with POTS and the variety of autonomic symptoms that patients experience, this medical oddity has gone by an assortment of additional names including dysautonomia, neurasthenia, hyperadrenergic orthostatic intolerance and chronic orthostatic intolerance.

Chapter 2 explains **How Blood Moves up to the Brain**

CHAPTER 2:

How Does Blood Move up to the Brain?

How Does Blood Move Around The Body?

The heart is the body's most important muscular pump with each beat propelling blood forward throughout the body. Each heart beat delivers life-sustaining oxygen and nourishing rich blood to the brain as well as all the tissues of the body. Many of the body's physiological processes normally work together as a team to move blood back to the heart, filling its chambers with blood for the next beat. Only a small percentage of the body's blood is positioned above the level of the heart. Blood above the level of the heart, primarily depends upon gravity alone to move that blood back down to the heart. As long as one keeps moving one's arms up and around, gravity helps direct that blood back to the heart. Valves within the veins of the arms prevent backwards flow. Whereas the majority (about 75%) of the body's blood is below the level of the heart, moving all of that fluid up against gravity back to the heart is a much more challenging task. Most four-legged animals don't share this problem as the majority of their blood is positioned above the level of the heart, not below.

Whereas the majority (about 75%) of the body's blood is below the level of the heart, moving all of that fluid up against gravity back to the heart is a much more challenging task. Most four-legged animals don't share this problem as the majority of their blood is positioned above the level of the heart, not below.

To better understand the pathways that blood travels throughout the body, let's look at the circulatory system. The tubes that blood travels within are called arteries and veins. Arterial blood delivers oxygen rich blood and nourishment from the heart to all the organs. Venous blood transports oxygen-poor blood back to the heart via veins. Venous System (**Figure 1**) illustrates the pathways of veins all transporting blood back to the heart. As blood travels in the veins back to the heart, the veins get increasingly larger. In contrast, the Arterial System (**Figure 2**) provides the pathways of arteries transporting blood away from the heart to all the organs of the body. As blood travels in the arteries from the heart, the arteries gradually decrease in size. Notice the placement of the heart up high in the body and the brain even higher up.

In between the arterial and venous systems is the Pulmonary System - where the right side of the heart delivers blood to the lungs and returns blood to the left side of the heart for general circulation. While blood is in the lungs, carbon dioxide (waste product of bodily metabolism) is exchanged for fresh oxygen (necessary for metabolism). Richly oxygenated blood is essential for the body's many metabolic processes.

Blood leaving the gastrointestinal organs delivers water, glucose and additional nutrients to the liver for processing, and eventually back to the heart.

Figure 1:

The Venous System

Pathways for Blood to Return from the Body's Organs to the Heart

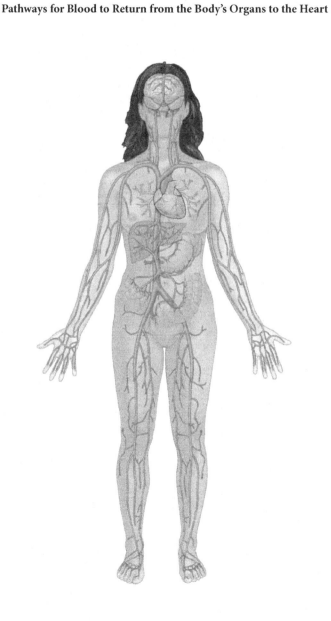

Figure 2:

The Arterial System

Pathways for Blood Leaving the Heart Going to the Body's Organs

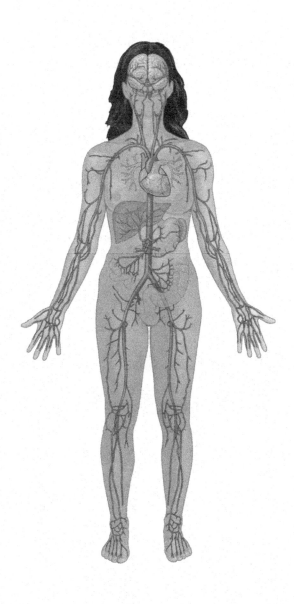

What Is The Role Of The Capillaries?

Capillaries are the smallest and thinnest blood vessels with only a single cell lining. Their size is about the same as that of a red blood cell, 7-8 micrometers (3/10,000 of an inch in diameter). That's one-tenth the thickness of a human hair. Capillaries are so tiny, that red cells must pass single file as they pass through the capillaries. The most important body processes take place within the networks of capillaries that connect the smallest arteries to the smallest veins. All bodily exchanges take place within these capillary networks - the transfer of gases, fluids and nutrients between the blood and tissues. Placed collectively end-end-to-end, the capillaries would stretch for more than 60,000 miles.

Within the capillaries of the lungs, red cells pick up oxygen to deliver to the tissues and carbon dioxide, the waste product of metabolism, is released into the air. Within the capillaries of the body tissues, essential oxygen, proteins, hormones and nutrients are delivered to the body's cells and waste products of metabolism pass into the bloodstream. In the liver and-kidneys, capillary-like networks are responsible for clearing the blood of waste products of metabolism and conserving essential nutrients. Glucose (sugar) can travel in both directions, depending on whether the body's need is for quick energy or energy storage. Glucose is mainly stored in the liver and some in the muscles for quick energy. As the muscle glucose is used up, more is mobilized from the liver serving as the energy warehouse.

How Does Blood Move Back to The Heart?

The contractions of the heart increase pressure within the major arteries and propel blood throughout the body. Arteries have thick muscular walls that stretch when the blood pressure reaches its peak and then contract to propel blood further along. Blood leaving the heart is propelled by this pressure. That pressure is measured in millimeters of mercury (mmHg). The mean arterial pressure of blood leaving the heart is approximately 100 mmHg. As blood travels through gradually smaller and smaller arteries the pressure gradually decreases. By time blood reaches the capillaries the mean pressure has fallen to 25-30 mmHg. From that point onward, the blood enters the venous system (related to veins). Because pressure within the venous system is even lower, more blood exists within the veins and blood moves much slower within the veins. About 75% of the body's blood is present within the veins at rest, waiting to return to the heart. Within the smaller veins the pressure is less than 10 mmHg and in the main vein leading to the heart, the pressure is barely measurable.

This presents the body with a major engineering problem - how to propel this vast quantity of blood uphill back to the heart. Standing requires complex physiologic mechanisms to move this increased quantity of blood from the lower body upward against gravity back to the heart. It would have been great, if we had mini-pumps within our big toes to propel this venous blood upward. But unfortunately, we were not created that way. So, the muscles of the lower extremities need to come to the body's rescue. In addition to moving the body, the leg muscles have an additional job – to squeeze the veins and massage the blood upward. Strategically placed valves assist by closing the veins, preventing blood from falling back downward. Why is all of this body physiology so important to POTS patients? Because, in order for the leg muscles to do their job, the muscles in the leg and veins need to be strong, salt content and blood volume need to be normal. And, that is exactly what's wrong with patients with POTS, leg veins are relaxed, both salt and blood volume are reduced.

Venous return, both during standing and exercising, requires proper functioning and coordination of multiple processes including:

- Venous valves – anti-gravity valves within extremity veins that prevent backflow
- Venous muscles – muscles within vein walls that can contract and move blood forward

- Thigh and Leg muscles – muscle contractions squeeze veins propelling blood forward

- Venous nerves – nerves that contract the muscles surrounding the veins

- Autonomic nervous system – recognizes the need to stimulate nerves and muscles

- Chest pump – inhalation increases negative chest pressure drawing blood to the heart

- Gravity – encourages return of blood from veins above the level of the heart

When exercising, the heart can pump out three times as much blood as during rest. Therefore, exercise requires peak performance of all venous components necessary to move blood upward.

All of us, with or even without POTS, depend upon this elaborate ingenious combination of bodily processes efficiently working together to accomplish the Herculean task of returning blood to the heart while standing. Even when healthy individuals assume the upright posture, gravity causes a redistribution of blood from the chest area towards the lower body. Even without POTS, three cups of blood shift toward the lower body (pooling into the abdomen, pelvis, thighs and legs) when standing or walking.

> It would have been great, if we had mini-pumps within our big toes to propel this venous blood upward. But unfortunately, we were not created that way. So, the muscles of the lower extremities need to come to the body's rescue. In addition to moving the body, the leg muscles have an additional job – to squeeze the veins and massage the blood upward.

Persistence of this increased pressure within the veins and capillaries of the lower body causes the legs to take on a purple-bluish hue. Over time, this increased capillary pressure within the legs forces fluid to leak out of the capillaries into the tissues. Leakage can cause swelling of the legs (edema). Shift of plasma fluid - loss from the vascular system into the adjacent tissues further decreases circulating blood volume – decreasing venous return to the heart, cardiac filling and outflow. This decrease in blood volume can be as great as 10%. Normally, while asleep (resting off of one's feet), this leg swelling is usually reabsorbed and excreted by the kidneys.

Why Are Veins In The Legs So Important?
Central in this process of venous return to the heart, is an adequately functioning venous system including intact valves, muscular walls and autonomic nerves all functioning properly to move blood back to the heart. Sympathetic nerves stimulate the muscles within the walls of veins telling them to contract (squeeze) and aid in directing blood toward the heart. Unlike the blood pressure within arteries that propels blood forward, the blood pressure within the veins is too low to propel blood.

As veins pass from the toes up the legs toward the heart, the veins become larger (increase in cross-sectional diameter), carry larger quantities of blood and the pressure gradually decreases to almost zero. To prevent gravity from pulling blood down the veins, nature has provided the veins with one-way valves. Valves act like little doors along the inner walls of the veins, opening to allow blood to flow upward, but closing when blood attempts to flow downward in the wrong direction. Venous valves are most plentiful in the lower legs. Because we don't have little pumps in our feet to force the blood up our long legs, we depend upon the contractions of the muscles of our lower extremities to constantly "squeeze, massage or pump" the blood up the leg veins from one set of valves to the next higher set of valves. Lower extremity muscular pumping (compression) of veins is the major mechanism responsible for moving blood present in the body below the level of the heart up against gravity back towards the heart. (**Figure 3**)

Figure 3:

**Coordinated Role of Leg Muscles
and Veins to Propel Blood Uphill Against Gravity.**

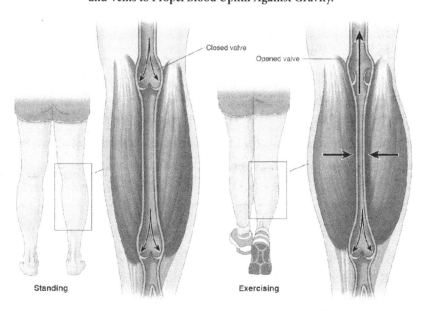

Closed valve   Opened valve

Standing   Exercising

Figure 3 illustrates the function of the valves of the veins. Open venous valves (on the right) are seen when contracting calf muscles massage blood up the legs during exercise. The closed venous valves (on the left) demonstrate how the resting leg muscles allow blood to accumulate in the leg veins when standing upright.

These illustrations demonstrate the coordinated role of leg muscles and veins to propel blood uphill against gravity. Because, at all times more blood in the body is physically below the level of the heart than there is above the heart, proper pumping function of all components is absolutely necessary to move adequate quantities of blood back to the heart. When upright, sympathetic stimulation of the muscles within the walls of the veins cause added contractions (squeezing and narrowing) – encouraging upward movement of blood.

As blood accumulates in the veins while standing still, pressure is placed on the venous veins stretching them above the valves. Over time, this stretching of the veins can widen the veins enough to make the valves ineffective and blood will leak downhill through the venous valves.

How Is Blood Volume Regulated?

Blood volume consists of plasma (liquid) and blood cells, amounting to about 5,000 ml (approximately 20 cups) in an adult. Females generally have smaller bodies and likewise have slightly smaller blood volumes. The body attempts to tightly control the blood volume by utilizing a number of mechanisms to adjust the volume. Fluids and salt ingested raise the blood volume, water and salt excreted by the kidneys into the urine lowers the blood volume. Body fluids are also lost via the skin, lungs and gastrointestinal tract. Optimally, the volume ingested and excreted is balanced. When all else fails, the kidneys come to the rescue. The kidneys regulate the amount of water and sodium excreted into the urine. When blood volume is excessive, the kidneys excrete more water and sodium. When the blood volume is reduced, the kidneys conserve sodium and water by reducing excretion into the urine.

The blood volume is distributed throughout the circulatory system. However, blood moves faster through the arteries and slower in the lower pressure veins. Consequently, approximately two-thirds of the circulating blood is retained within the venous vessels.

How Does the Heart Do Its Job?

The heart is an amazing organ, it automatically and alternately contracts and pumps blood. Then it relaxes and refills, bringing life-giving oxygen and nourishment to all the body's tissues. Each day the heart beats over 100,000 times and pumps 2,000 gallons of blood through 75,000 miles of blood vessels. During an average lifetime, the heart beats 2.5 billion times.

The role of a healthy well-conditioned heart is to receive the returning blood and with each subsequent contraction (heart beat), pump blood to the brain and all the rest of the body organs. Blood delivers life-sustaining oxygen and nourishment to all the body's organs 24 hours a day. Even when the normal heart is functioning at peak efficiency, only about half of the blood within the muscular heart is pumped out with each beat. The *percentage of blood* within the heart that is pumped out with each beat is called the *ejection fraction*. A normal *ejection fraction* would be 55-70%. Thus, normally about 55-70% of the blood within the heart is pumped out with each beat.

Measurement of the quantity of blood pumped out during each heartbeat is called the *stroke volume*. In adolescents the *stroke volume* measures approximately 3 ounces per beat (6 tablespoons), not that large an amount. The amount of blood pumped per minute by the heart is referred to as the *cardiac output. Cardiac output* is measured by multiplying stroke volume by heart beats per minute.

The role of a healthy well-conditioned heart is to receive the returning blood and with each subsequent contraction (heart beat), pump blood first to the lungs and then to the brain and all the rest of the body. It takes approximately one minute for blood to complete a cycle - leave the heart, circulate through the body and return to the heart. When necessary, like during exercise, blood can complete the cycle much faster. Blood delivers life-sustaining oxygen and nourishment to all the body's organs, but the brain remains most vulnerable to even subtle changes that diminish brain blood flow.

In healthy adolescents, about 3 ounces of blood is pumped out with each heartbeat (*stroke volume*). With a heart rate of 65 - 70 beats per minute, the cardiac output is approximately 200 ounces (24 cups)/minute. On a typical day, the heart pumps 2,000 gallons of blood. Because brain function is so important, cerebral (brain) blood flow (CBF) consists of 15% of the cardiac output whether awake or asleep. Nourishment of the brain amounts to about 3 ½ cups of blood per minute. Standing results in about a 10% reduction in CBF among normals, and in POTS patients the reduction can be as much as 20% - 30%. The brain is very dependent on a continuous supply of oxygen rich blood and glucose, and reduction in oxygenation interferes with normal brain function. Reduced cerebral blood flow results in an assortment of brain hypoperfusion (decreased blood supply) related-symptoms like headaches, drowsiness, visual disturbances, cognitive difficulties etc. If CBF falls by more than 50%, serious changes in consciousness can occur.

The heart is an amazing organ, it automatically and alternately contracts and pumps blood. Then it relaxes and refills, bringing life-giving oxygen and nourishment to all the body's tissues. Each day the heart beats over 100,000 times and pumps 2,000 gallons of blood through 75,000 miles of blood vessels. During an average lifetime, the heart beats 2.5 billion times.

How Does Breathing Effect Return of Blood to The Heart?

During relaxed abdominal breathing, with inspiration (inhaling) the diaphragm moves downward greatly enlarging the size of the chest cavity. Expansion of the chest produces a negative pressure within the chest. Negative lung pressure encourages air to enter the lungs and movement of blood within the veins leading to the heart to move more quickly - increasing venous return to the right heart and then the lungs. At the same time, the quantity of blood leaving the lungs going to the left heart decreases. Thus, temporarily right heart output increases and left heart output decreases. Stressful chest breathing is more rapid and requires more work.

During expiration (exhaling) the opposite occurs. Pressure within the chest cavity increases and blood within the veins entering the heart moves more slowly decreasing venous return to the right heart. When blood going to the lungs is diminished, the squeezing of the lungs forces blood into the left heart increasing cardiac output and generalized blood flow to the body.

Pressure changes associated with breathing enhance the movement of air into and out of the lungs. Breathing acts like a pump - alternately increasing return of blood to the right heart (during inspiration) and then increasing outflow from the left heart (during expiration).

Chapter 3 explains the **Causes of POTS (Orthostatic Intolerance)**

CHAPTER 3:

What Are the Causes of POTS (Orthostatic Intolerance)?

What Is Orthostatic Intolerance?

The cause of POTS is complex and cannot be attributed to any single factor. Normally, all of us can maintain active lifestyles and are able to stand upright, walk, play and work for prolonged periods of time without symptoms. Healthy non-POTS people are able to maintain an adequate flow of oxygen rich blood to the brain even during prolonged standing. Protection of the brain from reduced perfusion (nourishment) at all times is essential. Without adequate perfusion, the brain will suffer from cerebral anoxia (lack of oxygen).

During standing, POTS patients suffer from orthostatic intolerance, the occurrence of an assortment of bizarre symptoms when upright. When POTS patients are upright there is a reduction in the return of blood from the lower body to the heart and then recirculated to the brain and other vital organs. When one assumes the upright posture, gravity causes a shift in blood toward the lower limbs, placing a physiological challenge on the body's ability to maintain normal return of blood to the heart via the veins. Normally, in healthy individuals, about 25% -30% of the body's circulating blood is located in the mid-chest (heart and lungs). During standing upright, gravity will shift approximately 3 cups of this blood from the mid-body into the pelvis and legs – about 1 cup into the pelvis and 2 cups into the legs. Most of this gravitational shift takes place almost immediately after standing.

What Processes Go Wrong in POTS Patients?

Because of varying combinations of diminished circulating fluid volume, reduced salt intake, general physical deconditioning, heart muscle atrophy, venous stretching and circulatory malfunction, POTS patients are unable to overcome the physical stressors associated with the upright position. Unless remedied, this orthostatic intolerance consisting of blood pooling in the lower body results in a decreased quantity of blood available for each subsequent heartbeat.

The role of excessive venous pooling during standing has been confirmed by testing with red blood cells that have tagged (labelled) with radioactivity. Radioactivity in the calf region has been compared within healthy individuals while lying down and standing upright. Investigators tag red blood cells (add radioactivity to red blood cells), re-inject them and measure their circulatory paths. In healthy individuals, immediately upon assuming an upright posture, radioactivity (measured from radioactive tagged red blood cells) within the calf increases greater than 2-fold. Among POTS patients, the radioactivity increases almost 3-fold upon standing upright. Thus, in POTS patients, even more blood may gravitate into the lower abdomen, pelvis, thighs and legs during standing upright.

During orthostatic stress (standing upright) in individuals with POTS, there is exaggerated gravitational pooling of blood, a greater collection of blood in the lower abdomen, thighs and legs compared to people without POTS. Because there is reduced return of blood to the heart when upright, there is a subsequent reduced volume of blood pumped with each subsequent heartbeat (stroke volume). Specifically, during standing in individuals with POTS, the cardiac output is significantly reduced. The more severe the reduction in cardiac output and cerebral blood flow, the greater the cerebral oxygenation reduction and severity of symptoms.

Among normals (non-POTS patients), this pooling was confirmed 70 years ago by measuring the pressure within the veins of ankles during lying, sitting and standing. Venous pressure in the foot increased 5-fold when changing from lying to sitting and 8-fold after assuming a standing posture for 22 seconds. Walking on a treadmill resulted in a venous pressure of only 2-fold greater than lying and one-quarter of that measured during standing (a 4-fold fall during exercise). All of these measurements confirm the important role of muscular contractions of the leg muscles in pumping blood upward. Look what exercise can do! Exercise can even overpower the gravitational shifting of large quantities of blood within the body.

> During standing upright, gravity will shift approximately 3 cups of this blood from the mid-body into the pelvis and legs – about 1 cup into the pelvis and 2 cups into the legs. Most of this gravitational shift takes place almost immediately after standing.

Most adolescents who have not participated in regular strenuous exercise for a prolonged period of time develop weakened body muscles (the "use it or lose it" rule). This deconditioning takes place in the skeletal muscles and even the heart muscle. Sitting all day in classes and at the computer encourages the "use it or lose it" process. The deconditioning seen in POTS patients is similar to that seen after prolonged inactivity in bed or space flight. Lack of regular exercise and inactivity can be associated with heart deconditioning, atrophy of heart muscle (loss of muscle due to reduced use) with a resultant smaller sized heart. Atrophy of the heart muscle, often seen in individuals with POTS, further contributes to a reduced stroke volume. Today's adolescents spend too much screen time on computers, cell phones, watching television, doing homework and sitting in classes. Therefore, they are more prone to deconditioning or weakening of both their heart and leg muscles.

Why Is Reduced Circulating Blood Volume Important?

Many young people have low blood volume due to low intake of fluids and salt and reduced renin. Reduced circulating blood volume within the vascular system further diminishes blood flow in general, to and from the heart. Hypovolemia (low blood volume) is also seen following gastrointestinal disorders characterized by diarrhea (excess fluid loss) or nausea (reduced fluid intake). Hypovolemia combined with standing upright, as seen in those with POTS, results in an exaggerated increase in sympathetic outpouring of norepinephrine. This increase in norepinephrine increases the heart rate - a built-in mechanism designed to maintain adequate cardiac filling and output. Individuals who are experiencing rapid heart rhythm as well as other unexplained symptoms can also experience an increase in anxiety.

To complicate matters worse, among some POTS patients the veins of the lower body exhibit a dysautonomic response, that is they are unable to contract with sympathetic stimulation. The vein walls are unable to respond to the message to constrict and speed-up venous blood flow back to the heart. Why the veins fail to respond to the signal to constrict remains unclear.

Volume sensors within the kidneys help regulate fluid volume and blood pressure. When they detect reduced blood volume or blood pressure the hormone renin is released. The renin-angiotensin-aldosterone endocrine system increases reabsorption of salt and water by the kidneys, thus expanding blood volume. Among POTS patients, this renin-angiotensin-aldosterone system may be defective. Failure of this system adds to the diminished circulating fluid volume available to recirculate.

What Is the Heart's Role in Body Function?

The heart is a muscular organ that pumps blood to your entire body delivering oxygen and nutrients. Blood returning to the heart has a high content of carbon dioxide (a waste product of cell metabolism) that is exhaled (breathed out) by the lungs. In addition to the heart, arteries carry blood from the heart to the tissues of the body, and veins carry blood back to the heart. An electrical system controls your heart and uses electrical signals to contract the heart's chambers. The heart's pumping action is responsible for moving blood throughout the body.

> Many young people have low blood volume due to low intake of fluids and salt and reduced renin. Reduced circulating blood volume within the vascular system further diminishes blood flow in general, to and from the heart.

Reduced re-filling of the heart with blood from the veins, as seen with POTS - limits the heart's ability to provide blood to the upper body and especially the brain for nourishment. Reduced brain blood flow explains why POTS patients experience headaches, impaired cognition, short-term memory loss, weakness, dizziness, fatigue, drowsiness and visual disturbances while upright. Reduced return of blood to the heart initiates reflex tachycardia in an attempt to restore adequate return of blood to the brain. Tachycardia is often associated with an awareness of palpitations and skipped heart beats and anxiety.

Why Do I Feel Like I'm about to Pass-out?

All of us have seen young healthy soldiers who during standing at perfect attention without moving a muscle, suddenly collapse to the ground. All that's wrong with them is that they stopped massaging the blood in their lower extremities back to their heart, resulting in markedly diminished blood pressure and blood flow to the brain and loss of consciousness. In contrast, in POTS patients the blood pressure remains normal during standing, only the heart rate speeds up. Such blood pressure collapse with syncope (actual fainting) is not usually seen with POTS. Among POTS subjects, dizziness, lightheadedness and faint feelings are much more common than actual passing out. POTS patients may experience the sensation that they are about to pass-out (pre-syncope), but rarely do they actually pass-out (syncope).

Why Is Reduced Circulating Blood Volume So Important?

In patients with POTS during standing, the volume of blood returning to the heart is jeopardized. Thus, stroke volume (volume of blood pumped per beat), cardiac output (volume of blood pumped per minute) and cerebral blood flow (blood flow to the brain) are all reduced in sequence. When you start out with only 3 ounces of blood per beat, there is little room for significant reduction in the volume of blood pumped to the brain. In POTS patients the reduction in cerebral blood flow can be as large as 30%. The brain is very dependent on a continuous delivery of an adequate supply of oxygen rich blood, and reduction in oxygenation interferes with normal brain function. Reduced cerebral blood flow results in an assortment of brain hypoperfusion (decreased blood supply) related-symptoms like headaches, dizziness, drowsiness, visual disturbances, fatigue and cognitive difficulties.

How Does Physical Inactivity Cause Muscle Loss?

Physical deconditioning due to physical inactivity results in lower extremity and cardiac muscular atrophy (wasting and weakening), the old "use it or lose it" rule. In fact, many investigators believe that loss of heart muscle plays a major role in contributing to the symptoms of POTS. Dr. Benjamin D. Levine of Texas Health Presbyterian Hospital in Dallas, Texas has performed extensive research on the cardiac deconditioning seen among astronauts during space travel. The deconditioning observed after spaceflight is similar to that observed after prolonged bedrest. In fact, similar cardiac atrophy (loss of cardiac muscle due to deconditioning) has been observed among POTS patients, with females being the most vulnerable. Dr. Levine has even mentioned changing the POTS name to "Grinch Syndrome" (referring to the Dr. Seuss character with a "small heart"). Smaller hearts, as noted in many POTS patients, pump out less blood per beat. When combined with reduced circulating blood volume, as seen in most females – pooling of blood in the lower body results in decreased cardiac outflow and symptoms related to inadequate brain nourishment.

Why Is the Brain So Vulnerable to Diminished Blood Flow?

The brain, being the highest (placed physically at the top of body) and most complex structure in the body, is most vulnerable to decreased blood flow and oxygenated blood. In fact, many of the most disturbing symptoms associated with severe POTS are results of "brain steal" (insufficient blood flow to the brain due to shifting of blood downward) with compromised oxygen and essential nutrients. The brain's 200 billion nerve cells are interconnected and all depend on oxygen to perform their many complex functions. The more severe the "brain steal," the more severe are the resultant "brain-fog-related" POTS symptoms. In general, patients who experience symptoms of cognition impairment due to hypoperfusion (diminished blood flow) note that symptoms become more severe the longer one is upright and tend to only improve with lying down. When cognition is affected, thinking, learning and remembering become difficult.

Recently, antibodies to the signal receptors on the blood vessels of the lower extremities have been discovered in the blood of some POTS patients. What role these antibodies play in the blocking of the autonomic nervous system signals remains uncertain. One theory is that these antibodies are in response to recent infections and may be responsible for the reduced sympathetic constriction of the veins of the lower extremities when standing.

Do Giraffes Have POTS Symptoms?

If adolescents with POTS have difficulty maintaining a constant flow of blood to the brain, how do giraffes with long necks and legs avoid POTS-like symptoms? Giraffes grow to heights of 18 feet with 8-10 foot long necks. Do giraffes have POTS symptoms like lightheadedness, dizziness and mental cloudiness when moving their heads from drinking water in a river to suddenly raising their heads up to look up-over tops of trees for possible danger? POTS symptoms represent reduced blood flow to the brain, but giraffes don't seem to suffer from reduced blood flow to the brain. What protective mechanisms do giraffes have that POTS patients don't have?

To pump blood up to the brain of the tallest of land animals requires a huge heart, giraffe hearts weigh approximately 25 pounds, pumping blood at twice the pressure of humans. In contrast, an adult human heart weighs only 2/3 of a pound. Moreover, giraffes have a number of additional unique design features. The arteries of the long neck have special valves to divert blood into pockets when bending down to prevent the dangers associated with excessively high blood pressure within the blood vessels of the brain. The veins of the neck have both valves and muscles that limit downward flow when the head is upright. Best of all, nature has equipped their legs with "anti-gravity suits," thick tight-fitting skin and very strong muscles. All of these features are designed to prevent venous pooling and encourage venous return of blood to the heart. Thus, even with their tall bodies, giraffes don't have to worry about POTS symptoms.

Chapter 4 will explain **What Bodily Mechanisms Maintain Orthostatic Tolerance**

CHAPTER 4:

What Physiological Mechanisms Maintain Orthostatic Tolerance?

How Does The Body Control Blood Distribution?

The distribution of blood within the blood vessels is tightly controlled, but with enough flexibility to respond to a variety of challenges. Five quarts of blood loop through more than 60,000 miles of capillaries nourishing every cell of the body. However, at any one time some organs need more blood than others. To absorb nutrients following a heavy meal, the vessels of the abdominal organs dilate to increase the volume of available blood. When too hot, the vessels of the skin dilate (open) encouraging sweating and loss of heat. When too cold, the vessels of the skin constrict (narrow) discouraging loss of heat. When exercising vigorously, the vessels of the lungs and muscles dilate and the heart beats faster satisfying their need for greater blood flow. At the same time, the abdominal vessels constrict, reducing the available blood flow. Notice, the blood supply to the brain does not change unless upright posture shifts blood from the chest downward via gravitational action.

In addition to danger sensors within the brain, special stretch sensors (baroreceptors) within the major blood vessels of the neck are able to respond quickly to changes in blood volume and blood pressure by releasing adrenaline and norepinephrine. These stress hormones speed up the heart, constrict unessential blood vessels and prepare the body for battle.

Table 1: Percentages of Cardiac Output to Organs by Body Region and Activity Level

Regions	Organs	At Rest	Vigorous Exercising	Upright Posture
Brain	Brain	15 %	↑ 30 %	↓10-30 %
Chest	Lungs	25-30 %	↑ 3 fold	↓ 30 %
	Heart			
Abdomen	Intestines	30 %	↓ 50 %	↑ 30 %
	Liver			
	Kidneys			
Lower Leg Pelvis-Thigh	Muscles	17 %	↑ 25 fold	↑ 25 %

Table 1 displays the distribution of blood in the normal human body by region and activity level. Upon assuming the upright posture, gravity causes a shifting of 25-30 % of the blood progressively downward from the chest to the abdomen, pelvis-thigh and legs. Vigorous exercise shifts significant quantities of blood away from the abdominal organs to the heart, lungs and especially the muscles.

How Does The Body Cope With Orthostatic Stress (Standing Upright)?

When the body is upright, both during standing and walking, the circulatory system is most stressed. The body must find a way to move blood up from the legs against gravity. Returning blood from the legs back to the heart is a challenge - even among normal individuals. Returning blood from the legs back to the brain is - an even greater challenge. Rather than having diseased organs, POTS represents autonomic dysfunction - failure of several automatic bodily functions that are responsible for maintaining upward circulation while upright. Normal complex physiologic processes (automatic bodily functions) are responsible for returning blood from the lower body to critical organs like the heart and brain. When not functioning properly, as occurs in POTS patients, excessive blood accumulates in the lower abdomen and lower limbs rather than immediately returning to the heart to recirculate.

During orthostatic stress, the body has a number of auto-regulatory mechanisms that go into action to maintain a steady state. Cerebral (brain) sensors release norepinephrine, an adrenergic hormone signal, to speed up the heart rate and constrict the cerebral arteries. Even among healthy individuals, when blood flow to the brain (central nervous system) is diminished, like when assuming the upright posture, baroreceptors (low-pressure sensors (like thermostats) within neck blood vessels and heart chambers) recognize this reduction in flow. As flow falls, signals tell the brain to send messages to the heart to beat faster and contract the walls of the veins of the lower body. These muscular compressions of the veins act similarly to pinching the end of a garden hose with running water – the smaller the opening of the hose becomes, the faster the water flows. The resultant muscular narrowing of the veins encourages more rapid blood flow in the veins up towards the heart.

Table 2 compares:

> 1.) Normal physiological mechanisms associated with healthy bodily functions and
>
> 2.) Possible POTS symptoms associated with the impaired bodily functions (disturbed functions that cause symptoms when upright) that strive to maintain orthostatic tolerance (ability to stand upright without symptoms).

To fully appreciate the role each physiologic mechanism (bodily process) plays in both normal and POTS patients, *Start at the bottom of this Table and follow the step-wise flow of blood from legs to brain - the healthy and impaired functions and associated POTS findings.*

Table 2: Physiological Mechanisms That Maintain Orthostatic Tolerance

[Ability to Tolerate Standing and Walking Upright]

Symptoms Associated with Orthostatic Intolerance (POTS)

Physiological Mechanisms	Healthy Function	Impaired Function	POTS Findings
Cerebral Perfusion Supplying brain with oxygen & nourishment	Normal brain nourishment	Diminished blood supply to brain	Inattention, drowsiness, Light headed, dizziness Visual disturbances Altered mentation - brain fog Headaches - migraine-like
Sensors in neck arteries detect reduced cardiac output	Pulse raised, Leg veins constrict to protect brain blood supply	Pulse raised to protect brain from reduced blood supply	Rapid heart rate Heart palpitations Shortness of breath Rapid chest breathing Anxiety, sweating
Cardiac Output Heart pumping adequate blood to nourish body	Pumping of normal quantities of blood	Reduced output of blood from heart	Fatigue or weakness Low energy Exercise intolerance Fainting
Blood moves up the veins back to the heart against gravity	Normal return of blood to heart	Reduced return of blood to heart	Orthostatic intolerance (desire to lie down and avoid standing)
Muscles within veins squeeze blood up towards the heart	Muscles squeeze blood up veins back to the heart	Blood pools in veins of intestines	Nausea, bloating Vomiting, diarrhea Abdominal pain
Lower extremity muscles tighten [legs, thighs & fanny]	Muscles massage blood up the legs	Blood collects in veins of legs & lower abdomen	Fatigue or weakness Low energy Exercise intolerance Nausea, bloating Abdominal pain
Gravitational Shift Normal blood shift into lower body [@ 2 cups of blood]	Stresses vascular system	Excessive blood shift to veins of legs & lower abdomen	Bluish discoloration of legs Heaviness in legs Cold sweaty legs Tingling in fingers
Renin regulates salt and water reabsorption by the kidneys	Normal circulating blood volume	Reduced circulating blood volume	Dehydration Fatigue or weakness Low energy Exercise intolerance

When upright with healthy function, normal volumes of blood circulate, return to the heart, get pumped out, and nourish the brain adequately. This chart describes the physiological mechanisms (bodily processes) responsible for moving blood against gravity from the lower extremities via the heart all the way up to nourish the brain when upright. Sensors in the neck arteries have the responsibility to set off alarms when the supply of blood carrying oxygen and nourishment is compromised. The sympathetic nervous system sends signals to tell the heart to beat faster and the muscles within the walls of the veins in the lower extremities to contract. In addition, the out-pouring of renin by the adrenal glands tells the kidneys to reabsorb extra salt and water.

When upright with impaired function, reduced volumes of blood circulate. Reduced return of blood to the heart causes reduced blood pumped out and failure of adequate nourishment of the brain. With the impaired function seen among POTS patients, a variety of symptoms can result from each type of impaired function. Dehydration results in reduced circulating blood volume, weakness, low energy, exercise intolerance and fatigue. Excessive shifting of blood into the legs results in bluish discoloration, heaviness and cold sweaty legs. Excessive shifting of blood into the abdominal organs can result in nausea, bloating, diarrhea, vomiting and abdominal pain. Reduced cardiac output results in fatigue, weakness, fainting, low energy and exercise intolerance. "Brain steal" - diminished brain perfusion (nourishment) is responsible for headaches, dizziness, inattention, drowsiness, "brain fog" and visual disturbances.

> *Imagine being a popular athlete like Ira, age 18, who played competitive soccer and went to every weekend party. Over several months, he became so fatigued as to have difficulty leaving his room. He missed several days of school each week. Even when he went out to a movie with friends on a Saturday night, he couldn't recall anything about the movie on Sunday morning. His friends suspected he was*

either depressed or malingering. Because of his POTS, he had frequent lapses of memory, headaches and dizziness when upright. These are common examples of the "brain steal" symptoms observed among individuals with POTS. Movement of blood towards the lower body when upright, steals blood from feeding the brain of POTS patients.

Chapter 5 explains **Why POTS Patients Experience Such a Variety of Symptoms**

CHAPTER 5:

Why Do POTS Patients Experience Such a Variety of Symptoms?

What Symptoms Do POTS Patients Experience?

Patients with mild symptoms associated with standing may only experience heart racing, headaches and fatigue. The majority of POTS patients report having headaches. Headaches most often occur during standing (orthostatic headaches) and are frequently preceded by lightheadedness or dizziness. Headaches can take on a variety of forms. The pain may be localized - for example behind the eyes - or take on a migraine pattern with associated nausea, vomiting and vertigo. For some, the headaches occur daily, for others they occur erratically. For most the headaches and associated symptoms are more severe early in the day, for others they are worse as the day progresses.

Others complain additionally of light headedness, attention difficulties, or nausea when upright. Patients with more severe symptoms of orthostatic intolerance also complain of weakness, dizziness, frequent headaches, drowsiness, visual disturbances, diminished concentration, chest or abdominal pain, rapid heart rate or shortness of breath. Most patients have their own unique group of recurring symptoms.

When upright with impaired
function, reduced volumes of blood
circulate. Reduced return of blood
to the heart causes reduced blood
pumped out and failure of adequate
nourishment of the brain.

Are My Body Changes Correctable?

Rather than disease of an organ, the multiple bizarre symptoms associated with POTS are caused by altered body physiology (function), "brain steal" (blood diverted away from the brain) brought on by standing among individuals with correctable body changes. The following is a list of the many possible correctable body changes and the resultant alterations in body physiology that have been observed in individuals with POTS:

Table 3: How to Minimize the Physical Consequences of POTS

Physical Consequences of Having POTS	What You Can Do to Minimize the Symptoms of POTS
Diminished circulating blood volume	Increase fluid intake
	Increase salt intake
Loss of skeletal muscle (deconditioning)	Increase physical activity*
Weakening of heart muscle (deconditioning)	
Gravitational pooling of blood toward the lower body and legs	Increase leg muscle conditioning
Venous dilatation of lower body	Increase contractions of muscles surrounding the veins in the legs
Rapid heart rate	Decrease nervous system activation
Excessive fatigue	Increase amount of restful sleep
Stress symptoms	Increase relaxation techniques and abdominal breathing

*Physical deconditioning due to lack of physical activity results in lower extremity and cardiac muscle atrophy (wasting and weakening), the old "use it or lose it" rule.

Each individual with POTS has her/his own combination of correctable body changes. Therefore, it is important to seek the help of a POTS medical specialist to design a personalized **"Guide to Recovery"** program. Most alterations in body physiology responsible for reducing the return of blood from the lower body to the heart and brain are correctable.

Rather than disease of an organ, the multiple bizarre symptoms associated with POTS are caused by altered body physiology (function), "brain steal" (blood diverted away from the brain) brought on by standing among individuals with correctable body changes.

What Activities Aggravate POTS Symptoms?

Symptoms of autonomic imbalance may be exaggerated following showering, particularly a hot shower, low-grade exercise, lack of sleep, physical fatigue, heat exposure, caffeine and diuretic ingestion. Many adolescent girls report worsening of symptoms during menses. Even eating heavy meals can aggravate POTS symptoms because blood is diverted to the abdominal organs during digestion - further reducing circulating blood volume. Dehydration may contribute to many of these conditions that aggravate POTS symptoms. In some patients, symptoms may be made worse while going up in an elevator, flying in an airplane or riding a roller coaster. Activities such as these have been known to encourage shifting of blood towards the lower body.

What Are The Symptoms Of Brain Hypoperfusion (Decreased Blood Flow)?

Some of the symptoms associated with brain hypoperfusion (decreased blood flow) have taken on distinctive characteristics resulting in unique descriptive names. A unique headache seen with brain hypoperfusion of POTS is the "coat-hanger headache" pattern (pain in the back of the head, neck and shoulders). A unique visual disturbance seen with POTS is tunneling (narrowing of the visual field like looking through a tube) referred to as the "Alice-in-Wonderland" pattern. And of course, most patients report that their symptoms improve by lying down. Individuals also complain of headaches over an eye on one side of their head resembling a typical migraine headache.

POTS patients with serious brain anoxia (lack of oxygenated blood), find POTS both incapacitating and frightening to themselves and their family members. Severe orthostatic intolerance causes profound reduction of perfusion of blood to the brain -"brain steal" with resultant "brain fog" and a strong urge to lie down. Impaired brain cognitive functioning or "brain fog" consists of difficulty thinking, focusing and communicating, confusion and being forgetful. The most frightening symptom is short-term memory loss, the inability to recall relatively recent, but significant events and experiences. Some of these patients even fear they may have early onset of Alzheimer's disease. Impaired nourishment of the brain's visual centers results in a variety of disturbances of vision including blurring, blind spots and rarely even temporary loss of vision.

As a result of brain fog or cognitive impairment, patients experience significant functional limitations. Activities associated with daily living may become severely limited. Thus, schoolwork, shopping, productivity and quality of life deteriorate. Academic, vocational and economic advancements suffer. Social activities like dating, attending theater, concerts and sporting events become unworkable.

Jenna, a 17 year old, didn't know that standing shifts 2 or more cups of blood into the lower body, steals that blood from the brain and causes the symptoms associated with POTS. Jenna had to learn to put-up with morning headaches, dizziness, shoulder pain, tunnel vision (like looking through a tube) and difficulty concentrating. Even slight exertion was associated with feelings of exhaustion. For Jenna, her most terrifying symptom was short-term memory loss. She feared she was "going crazy!" During an agonizing 3 years, she experienced many frightening occurrences of "brain fog" including the following:

- *Preparing to take a shower, she was shocked to discover her hair had been cut the day prior, but she had no recall of the event.*

- *When asked about her one- hour consultation with a psychiatrist, she was shocked to discover she had absolutely no recall of that prior day meeting.*

- *Classmates repeatedly complained about the number of times they had to convey assignments to her, because she would frequently have no recall of those discussions.*

Jenna's friends began to think that she was faking her symptoms to get more attention.

Does Bed Rest Help POTS Patients?

Many patients with POTS learn to avoid the symptoms associated with standing by lying down. Some spend a considerable part of each day resting in bed. Unfortunately, excessive bed rest encourages added unhealthy muscular deconditioning with bodily changes that actually worsen the symptoms associated with POTS. Excessive bed rest and lack of exercise promote atrophy (loss) and weakening of heart and skeletal muscles, reduced blood volume and impaired lower extremity venous muscular pumping - all factors that can lead to worsening of symptoms.

> *Sharon is 38 year-old mother of 2 adolescents with a year-long history of chronic fatigue, headaches, dizziness, muscle and joint pains. It all began following a flu-like illness with several days of fever, headache and generalized body aching. Since, she has suffered with progressive and increasingly severe exhaustion. Her arms and legs constantly feel heavy and painful. The slightest activity causes worsening of her fatigue. Rest and sleep do not provide improvement. When standing, whether in the kitchen or just talking, she soon gets lightheaded and dizzy with blurred vision and must lie down immediately to prevent mental confusion. She is no longer able to care for her family or prepare meals. She rarely leaves her home. Fortunately, her husband works from home and is able to take over the domestic responsibilities. Recently she was diagnosed with Chronic Fatigue Syndrome with POTS.*

Is POTS Always Bad?

Many more adolescents and young adults have a milder form of POTS that may never be recognized. Probably, a significant percentage of these patients with mild POTS during adolescence will eventually outgrow their autonomic dysfunction (abnormal automatic bodily functions). As they grow older, the autonomic nervous system catches up with the sky-scraper body growth spurt, the automatic functions mature and POTS can self-correct. "Mother Nature" and "Father Time" can often combine and become the "Best Doctors," healing many troubling conditions over time, even POTS.

Additional criteria required to establish the diagnosis of POTS include the presence of symptoms related to gravitational shifting of blood to the lower body, decreased cardiac output and sympathetic nervous over activity.

To establish a diagnosis of POTS, symptoms would have occurred frequently or constantly or fluctuate from day to day or week to week and need to have been present for at least 3- 6 months. Milder POTS patients experience the same common symptoms like fatigue, headaches, light-headedness, eye and abdominal disturbances, just milder.

POTS patients with serious brain anoxia (lack of oxygenated blood), find POTS both incapacitating and frightening to themselves and their family members. Severe orthostatic intolerance causes profound reduction of perfusion of blood to the brain -"brain steal" with resultant "brain fog" and a strong urge to lie down. Impaired brain cognitive functioning or "brain fog" consists of difficulty thinking, focusing and communicating, confusion and being forgetful.

What Pain Do POTS Patients Experience?

POTS patients frequently experience chronic pain. The most common pain complaint is headache. POTS-related headaches are caused by diminished blood supply to the brain and diminished cerebrospinal fluid bathing the brain due to dehydration. Less frequent types of pain are abdominal and rib cage pain. Other than rib cage joint pains, extremity joint pains are not part of the pure POTS pattern. Some POTS patients notice chest pains associated with their rapid and/or irregular heartbeats. More recently, it has been recognized that 2/3 of patients meeting the criteria for POTS also report abdominal complaints. POTS combined with abdominal pain occurs most frequently among young girls.

Venous blood pooling of the abdominal organs occurs along with venous pooling of the legs during an orthostatic challenge (standing upright). The abdominal organs consisting of the liver, stomach, intestines, pancreas and spleen contain considerable quantities of venous blood. In fact, 25-30% of the body's blood can be found within the abdominal organs at rest. Both eating a large meal and standing can increase the blood volume within the abdominal organs. The stress associated with this excessive abdominal pooling of blood results in removal of a significant quantity of blood from the general circulation. With less blood available to return to the heart, POTS symptoms may worsen.

How these changes upset abdominal function and worsen POTS abdominal symptoms are still not clear. It is suspected that the increased venous pooling of blood alters intestinal nerve function of the stomach, small and large intestine. These altered nerve signals result in abnormal intestinal motility (movement of digesting food), either more rapid or more delayed intestinal transit. More often the passage of digesting food is speeded up resulting in nausea, diarrhea and abdominal pain. Less frequently the passage of digesting food is slowed down resulting in bloating, vomiting, abdominal pain and constipation.

POTS patients with predominantly abdominal symptoms suffer primarily with nausea, vomiting and abdominal pain, but can also experience early fullness, cramping, bloating, diarrhea or constipation. POTS patients with the severest nausea and abdominal pain avoid eating and tend to lose weight. Patients with the severest weakness, fatigue and abdominal distress are forced to seek relief by avoiding standing situations and spend most of the day lying down.

Characteristically, during prolonged standing the lower legs feel cool and moist to touch and take on a purplish-blue discoloration (due to gravitational venous blood puddling). Greater venous pooling can result in heaviness within the legs, but not leg joint pains.

What Is the Role of Other Gastrointestinal Disorders?

Many gastrointestinal disorders are accompanied with diarrhea. Diarrhea causes loss of fluids, nutrients and electrolytes (salts). A variety of chronic intestinal disorders with diarrhea as a symptom are common among young adults. The most frequent of these disorders are: irritable bowel syndrome (IBS), inflammatory bowel disease (IBD), cystic fibrosis, celiac disease (gluten intolerance), lactose intolerance, ulcerative colitis and even medications (laxatives, caffeine, thyroid hormone and antibiotics). The first two, IBS and IBD, occur primarily among young females. Diagnosing both conditions is frequently difficult as testing is unreliable.

Having both POTS and one of these gastrointestinal disorders with chronic diarrhea can make management of POTS most difficult. Whether the diarrhea occurs intermittently or chronically, when present, diarrhea results in significant fluid and salt loss and reduction of circulating blood volume (hypovolemia). POTS patients are particularly vulnerable when diarrhea strikes. When a POTS patient experiences diarrhea, whatever the cause, hypovolemia accelerates and POTS symptoms will worsen.

When POTS patients have any of the disorders that can cause bouts of diarrhea, they need to learn about the importance of associated fluid and salt loss. They need to have ready-to-implement plans for substantially increasing fluid and salt intake. They must learn to replace more fluids and salts then are lost within the diarrhea, or they may find themselves needing to go to an Emergency Room for intravenous fluids and salt replenishment.

How Do the Adrenal Glands and Kidneys Prevent Low Blood Volume?

When necessary, small adrenal glands located on top of each kidney release adrenaline to increase the heart rate. This surge in heart rate is the body's attempt to correct the reduced heart output and protect the brain from reduced nourishment. Both of these auto-regulatory functions serve together to maintain blood flow and pressure within the brain's blood vessels and protect the brain from anoxia (lack of oxygen) during ortho-static stress.

Volume sensors within the kidneys also help regulate fluid volume and blood pressure. With prolonged standing, these sensors detect reduced blood volume and renin is released. The renin-angiotensin-aldosterone endocrine system (RAA) increases reabsorption of salt and water by the kidneys, thus increasing blood volume. Some evidence exists that the RAA system may be malfunctioning in some POTS patients.

Why Do POTS Patients Go So Long without Help?

Each POTS patient experiences their own unique set of orthostatic-related symptoms. Subsequently, each patient presents to a health care provider with a unique complex set of symptoms that don't match common dis-ease entities. Unfortunately, POTS is unknown to the majority of medical practitioners. In addition, routine physical examinations do not provide clues that support any recognized medical condition. Thus, most POTS patients go from medical specialist to specialist for months, years or even decades before discovering the actual cause of their puzzling chronic and unexplained symptoms. All of these trips to multiple doctors and medical centers for more and more tests can also add a significant financial burden to an already stressed family. Even following exclusion of many common as well as rare medical conditions, rarely is POTS considered as a possible cause of this unusual symptom complex. Consequently, otherwise healthy appearing adolescents and young adults suffering with POTS go from doctor to doctor without getting the help they need.

Are POTS Symptoms Always Severe?

The distribution of most characteristics and events in nature fit into a typical pattern referred to as the "Bell Shaped Curve." (See **Figure 4**). It's called a "Bell Shaped Curve" because when events fit into a normal distribution and are plotted on graph paper the shape of the curve resembles a bell. For example, if you plot the frequency of totals from rolling 2 standard 6-sided dice 100 times, the results will be pretty much the same each time. At one end of the curve will be a few 2s (two ones) and at the other end will be a few 12s (two sixes). The total 7 will be in the middle and be the tallest (most frequent result). The frequency of the other rolls will fall in between. Casinos capitalize on this higher frequency of rolling 7's (more combinations total seven) in the game of craps to stack the odds against gamblers (in craps a 7 loses).

Figure 4: Dice Rolls Form Bell Shape Curve

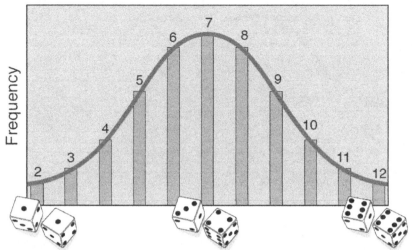

Dice Rolls Form Bell Shape Curve

If one plots the frequency of cases of POTS by severity, the results will also "resemble a bell curve." But, not all frequency plots are perfectly symmetrical. In fact, if there are more patients with milder symptoms the curve (bell) will need to shift to the left. (See **Figure 5**) More patients with severe symptoms shifts the curve (bell) to the right.

Figure 5: Distribution of POTS Cases by Severity

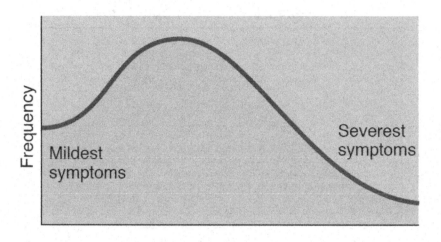

It seems that those with the severest symptoms are the most recognizable as POTS, but fortunately they do not make up the majority of cases.   It is generally believed that patients with the mildest symptoms outnumber those with severe symptoms. Many more adolescents and young adults have a milder form of POTS. In fact, many cases are so mild as to never be recognized as POTS. Probably, a significant percentage of patients with mild POTS during adolescence self-correct with time. They eventually outgrow their autonomic dysfunction (abnormal automatic bodily functions). As they grow older, the autonomic nervous system catches up with the skyscraper body growth spurt, the automatic functions mature and POTS can self-correct. "Mother Nature" and "Father Time" can often combine and become the "Best Doctors," healing many troubling conditions over time, even POTS.

What Is Medicine Doing to Figure Out What Is Wrong with Me?

Beginning in the mid-1900s, sporadic reports started appearing in medical journals describing cases of postural anxiety, rapid heartbeat (tachycardia), fatigue and dizziness among otherwise healthy young adults. These cases were labeled as neurocirculatory asthenia or dysautonomia (automatic circulatory control abnormalities). In 1993, Drs. Ronald Schondorf and Phillip A. Low at the Mayo Clinic in Rochester, MN were the first to report on performance of tilt tests on a group of primarily young women labeled as having psychological-induced fatigue. They determined that these young adults had rapid pulse rates within minutes of being tilted upright and demonstrated orthostatic intolerance (inability to stand upright) without symptoms. These young women reported tachycardia, fatigue and lightheadedness. The Mayo Group referred to this condition as *idiopathic postural orthostatic tachycardia syndrome* or POTS (idiopathic meaning without a known cause). The major distinguishing characteristic was tachycardia without significant change in blood pressure upon standing upright (orthostatic intolerance), in otherwise healthy young individuals. The mechanisms responsible for this mystifying illness remained a mystery for many years.

Currently almost fifty articles appear in medical journals each year reporting on studies of POTS by medical investigators from around the world. This suggests a worldwide epidemic and actually it confirms greater frequency of occurrence and recognition.

Based on this extensive research, we are learning more and more about the common symptom patterns experienced by those who suffer with POTS and methods for correcting the abnormal body changes. Mechanisms and how to manage the treatment of POTS have been mostly elucidated during the last 10 years. This book summarizes the essential facts necessary to understand the altered body physiology responsible for the multiple bizarre symptoms associated with POTS and what is required to overcome its troubling symptoms.

Chapter 6 explains the **Role of the Autonomic Nervous System (ANS)**

CHAPTER 6:

What Is the Role of the Autonomic Nervous System (ANS)?

Who Needs An Automatic Nervous System?

The autonomic (automatic) nervous system (ANS) is responsible for maintaining homeostasis (equilibrium) of the body's inner organs no matter the stressor. The ANS controls all the body functions that work on auto-pilot like heartbeat, breathing, digestion, eye muscles and endocrine glands. The controls of the ANS never sleep. Their job is to promote calm when appropriate and when necessary, activate protective responses to danger. They do their work by monitoring our inner body and its surroundings and controlling blood flow via small blood vessel dilatation (widening) and constriction (narrowing). ANS signals control heart rate, breathing, metabolism, digestion, vision and sexual function. They control sweat, salivary and tear glands and adjust body temperature. Signals from these nerves continuously fine tune adjustments to our environment.

The ANS controls all functions automatically without conscious input. Therefore, the autonomic nervous system is also referred to as the unconscious nervous system. When the ANS malfunctions, it is called dysautonomia (autonomic dysfunction). Approximately 2-3 percent of the US

population and 4% of children and adolescents have disordered au
function. Most of these do not have POTS. Instead, they have othe
ders of autonomic dysfunction.

***

It is generally believed that patients
with the mildest symptoms outnumber
those with severe symptoms. Many more
adolescents and young adults have a
milder form of POTS. In fact, many cases
are so mild as to never be recognized as
POTS. Probably, a significant percentage
of patients with mild POTS during
adolescence self-correct with time.

***

On the other hand, the voluntary nervous system, completely under an
individual's control, controls our voluntary movements. Groups of opposing muscles voluntarily activate bodily movements. For example flexors
bend arms and legs and extensors straighten arms and legs.

ANS centers within the brain also sense and respond to stress, emotions,
hunger and thirst. To finely tune the performance of the body's many
parts requires two major divisions performing opposite reflex functions.
One division is the sympathetic nervous system (SNS) and the other is
the parasympathetic nervous system (PNS). Both opposing divisions have
sensory components listening in on our external environment and inner
body functions and action components to make the necessary adjustments
required to maintain homeostasis (a resting state).

Epinephrine and norepinephrine are the signal transmitters of the sympathetic nervous division and acetylcholine is the signal transmitter of the parasympathetic nervous division.

It is of utmost importance to maintain adequate flow of blood to the brain. Unlike other medical conditions among adults like strokes, excessive blood loss and heart disorders that can cause permanent brain damage, POTS in otherwise healthy young adults is not known to cause permanent brain damage.

When all other systems falter, it is the responsibility of the autonomic nervous system to immediately step in and rescue the brain from an inadequate blood supply. All actions are attempts to correct the deficit in blood returning to the heart.

What Does The Sympathetic Nervous Division (SNS) Do?

The sympathetic nervous division has been described as the emergency defense system that turns on the "fright, fight or flight" response when provoked by danger. Preparation for battle demands a faster and stronger heartbeat, dilatation of the arteries feeding the skeletal muscles (increasing blood supply to the muscles for immediate action), enlargement of the airways of the lungs (more oxygen) and release of stored glucose from the liver for immediate energy. To see the enemy better, the pupils dilate and eyelids elevate. Whereas we depend on the skeletal muscles receiving maximum blood to save us from imminent danger, we prepare to fight or flee by tensing up. At the same time, the SNS messengers cause narrowing of the arteries feeding the salivary, abdominal digestive and sexual organs. This later group of organs plays no role in survival from danger; therefore, they are turned off temporarily.

The emergency sympathetic activity is turned on in response to a variety of stressors. Since the days of the cavemen, the stress response has served a useful function, to save us from physical dangers. Activation of the sympathetic response results in secretion of epinephrine and norepinephrine (stress hormone messengers). Epinephrine comes from the adrenal glands and norepinephrine from the sympathetic nerves. Pouring out of these hormones into the general circulation quickly prepares us to be battle-ready or to flee. Unfortunately, today we experience more emotionally-induced stressors than physically-induced dangers. In fact, emotional stressors are more likely to persist for longer periods of time than physical stressors. Thus, prolonged emotional stressors can result in a persistent state of hypervigilance (preparedness for battle), including generalized tightness of muscles and eventual exhaustion.

In addition to centers in the brain, sympathetic nerves originate from a chain of ganglia (bundles of nerves) connected to the spinal cord along each side of the spine. Nerves that go from these bundles of nerves have a positive impact on eyes, lungs, heart, muscles and liver and negative impact on digestive secretions and voiding.

What Does The Parasympathetic Nervous Division (PNS) Do?

The ganglia for the parasympathetic nervous system are located close to or within the affected organs. The parasympathetic nervous system (calming nervous system) secretes acetylcholine to activate its actions. It is responsible for maintaining normal function of the internal organs. Acetylcholine slows the heart and breathing rates, increases secretion of saliva, gastrointestinal motility and digestion. The PNS constricts the pupils. PNS activation keeps all the internal organs running smoothly. In contrast to the SNS, the PNS maintains the body in a state of calmness and participates in sexual arousal.

What Are The Autonomic Nervous System Responses To Orthostatic Stress?

The body depends on the autonomic nervous system to rescue it from reduced circulating blood volume as occurs in POTS. Restoring equilibrium and maintaining blood flow to the critical organs, especially the brain is essential. In patients with POTS, baroreceptors (pressure sensors) within the aorta and carotid arteries in the neck detect diminished blood flow to the brain and baroreceptors within the large veins leading to the heart can detect reduction in venous return to the heart. Whereas both occur in POTS patients during standing, these sensors turn on sympathetic signals that promote recovery. Baroreceptors within the arteries leaving the heart also relay sympathetic signals to the adrenal gland to secrete extra adrenalin (epinephrine).

Higher levels of norepinephrine secreted by sympathetic nerves and the adrenal glands attempt to rescue the brain from lack of oxygen. This strong cardiovascular stimulant both speeds up the heart rate as well as constricts the veins of the lower body. Secretion of elevated norepinephrine levels may also be responsible for heart palpitations, anxiety and trembling, sweating, shortness of breath, dilated pupils and elevation of blood pressure.

Collectively, these hormones turn on a number of sympathetic reflexes designed to restore homeostasis. Working as a team, both arms of the ANS work together to control the heart rate. When the sympathetic component is turned on (speeding up the heart rate) in POTS patients, the parasympathetic slowing component is turned off (also speeding up the heart rate). Together, all these members of the autonomic nervous system team perform as designed, increasing cardiac output and maintaining blood flow to all critical organs, especially the brain.

Chapter 7 explains **The Clues to Diagnosis of POTS**

What Are the Clues to A Diagnosis of POTS?

Why Is It So Difficult to Diagnose POTS?

Clues to a diagnosis of POTS consist of symptoms (complaints from the patient) and signs (observations made by a medical professional). If only a "routine" physical examination with routine laboratory tests is performed, specific clues pointing to a diagnosis of POTS will certainly not be found.

Why is it that POTS patients go to health care providers complaining of a multitude of bizarre symptoms such as headaches, fatigue, lightheadedness, rapid heart, blurry vision and abdominal pain without their POTS ever being suspected? Misdiagnosis and delay is so typical for POTS. In fact, Dysautonomia International reports that the average delay in establishing a POTS diagnosis is almost 6 years. One important reason is that performance of routine physical examinations and routine screening laboratory tests will always fail in providing clues as to the responsible diagnosis, POTS. None of these exams or tests will suggest the proper diagnosis. Suspicion of the diagnosis comes from taking a very extensive history of the patient's bizarre story and suspecting POTS as a possible cause.

Diagnosing POTS requires paying close attention to the patient's story - every little detail, every subtle symptom, and every subtle sign.

Performance of the special HUTT (Head-Up Tilt Test) that can reveal the onset of rapid heart rate upon assuming the upright posture would be helpful, but it is not readily available to most physicians.

Onset of Illness & Tests

Max at age 13 started complaining of headaches, dizziness and "tunnel vision" when standing up from the breakfast table. After breakfast, he developed strong feelings that he needed to go back to bed, because he didn't think he could handle school that day. He consulted a neurologist that specialized in teenagers with migraine headaches. Her working diagnosis was migraines. At that time, he had extensive testing that included:

- *Countless blood tests (including negative Lyme disease titers)*
- *Electroencephalogram (brain waves)*
- *Eye examinations by a retina specialist*
- *Neuro-ophthalmologist (brain-eye specialist)*
- *MRI (magnetic resonance imaging) of brain and neck*

All of these tests came back normal. His biggest problem remained that, "Nobody believed that he was really sick!" Subsequently, 3 years later he was diagnosed with POTS after another neurologist requested a Head-Up Tilt Test.

What Clues Suggest POTS?

The orthostatic symptoms observed among POTS patients are associated with decreased stroke volume and subsequently, decreased brain flow. Similar symptoms can also be observed among healthy individuals following extended periods of bed rest, viral illnesses and recovery from surgery. Many of us have experienced that sensation of feeling faint or passing out when attempting to stand during a severe viral or intestinal infection. Many POTS patients report worsening of symptoms following heavy meals, light exercise, during hot weather and menses. Some associate increased symptoms with the Valsalva maneuver (see the **How to Test for POTS Chapter 8**) which is associated with coughing, moving one's bowels and resistance exercise (weight lifting). These maneuvers temporarily increase pressure within the chest, temporarily diminishing venous return to the heart.

POTS is differentiated from other forms of orthostatic tachycardia by the ability of this group of patients to maintain normal blood pressure during standing. Blood pressure may rise or fall, but only minimally when upright. Blood pressure does not fall significantly during standing. When blood pressure falls significantly during standing that is known as orthostatic hypotension (standing low blood pressure). Orthostatic hypotension can be associated with many other medical conditions, but generally not with POTS.

What Are My POTS Symptoms?

The following checklists present the many symptoms reported by patients with POTS. The more symptoms reported, the more likely POTS may be the cause of your mysterious illness. Check off the frequency boxes of those symptoms you have experienced and share their frequency with your personal physician. Also, grade the symptom severity by circling your most severe and disturbing symptoms.

Patients with POTS can experience all of the symptoms in the lists that follow. But, no one patient has all of these signs and symptoms described here. Each patient has their own unique combination of symptoms. Most POTS patients report having many of the symptoms found in these lists in varying degrees of severity and at variable times. Share your lists with your healthcare providers.

Symptoms Reported By Patients With POTS – Check off Yours

Table 4: Hyperadrenergic Symptoms – Secretion of epinephrine and nor-epinephrine (stress hormone messengers) into the circulation to prepare the body for action produces the following symptoms. POTS patients report the following stress hormone related symptoms:

Hyperadrenergic Symptoms	FREQUENCY				
	Almost all the time	Very often	Often	Sometimes	Never
Tachycardia when upright					
Heart palpitations					
Irregular heartbeat					
Anxiety					
Chest pain/ discomfort					
Shortness of breath					
Clamminess					
Tremulousness					
Dilated pupils					
Warm feeling					

Table 5: Generalized Symptoms – POTS patients report the following generalized symptoms:

Generalized Symptoms	FREQUENCY				
	Almost all the time	Very often	Often	Sometimes	Never
Fatigue					
Weakness					
Low energy					
Daytime tiredness					
Exercise intolerance					
Standing intolerance					
Trembling					
Reduced hours upright during the day					
Anxiety					
Sleep disturbance					
Daytime sleepiness (need to nap)					
Trouble falling asleep					
Unrefreshing sleep					
Restless sleep					
Sweating					
Aches and pains					

Table 6: Venous Pooling Symptoms – Pooling of blood into the lower extremities results in over-stretching and congestion of the veins and delay of blood returning to the heart. POTS patients report the following pooling-related symptoms after standing for a period of time.

Venous Pooling	FREQUENCY				
	Almost all the time	Very often	Often	Sometimes	Never
Coldness of legs or feet					
Bluish discoloration of legs					
Bluish discoloration of feet					
Moist legs or feet when upright					
Skin of hands cold and sweaty					
Skin of legs cold and sweaty					
Swelling of legs					
Heaviness in the legs					
Paleness in face					

Table 7: Brain Hypoperfusion Symptoms – Diminished cerebral blood flow limits the delivery of life-sustaining oxygen and nourishment to the brain. POTS patients report the following symptoms related to reduced blood flow to the brain:

Brain Hypoperfusion	FREQUENCY				
	Almost all the time	Very often	Often	Sometimes	Never
Prolonged fatigue					
Exhaustion					
Weakness					
Migraine-like headaches					
Visual disturbances					
Disorientation/ confusion					
Blurring of vision					
Tunneled vision					
Temporary loss of vision					
Drowsiness					
Dizziness					
Lightheadedness					
Feeling faint					
Desire to lie-down					
Avoiding standing					
Cognitive difficulty					
Poor concentration					
Foggy thinking					
Difficulty focusing					
Forgetfulness					
Short-Term Memory loss					

Table 8: Gastrointestinal Dysfunction Symptoms – Pooling of blood and stretching of the veins draining the gastrointestinal organs can result in inflammation and disturbed motility function (movement of contents). Two-thirds of POTS patients have disturbed stomach emptying. Rapid emptying is more common than slowed emptying. POTS patients report the following abdominal symptoms.

Gastrointestinal Symptoms	FREQUENCY				
	Almost all the time	Very often	Often	Sometimes	Never
Nausea					
Vomiting					
Bloating					
Diarrhea					
Constipation, irregular bowel habits					
Abdominal pain after large meals					
Abdominal pain while standing					
Abdominal cramping					

What Can We Learn From Published Medical Reports?

Most published medical reports discuss the various symptoms experienced by patients with POTS. However, few publications actually performed surveys and analyzed their results. **Table 9** presents the comparative data from 5 such available articles. Interestingly, almost 90% of patients described in these 5 articles were females.

Table 9: POTS Symptoms – Survey-Based Analyses

Study	1	2	3	4	5
Participants	39	152	37	900	84
Females (%)	34 (89%)	132 (87%)	29 (88%)	-	73 (87%)
Mean Age (years)	35	30	15	-	25
Frequency (%)					
Palpitations	92	75		92	81
Fatigue	90	48		97	74
Weakness		50		88	41
Headache (orthostatic)	87		89		66
Headache (migraine)	28	28	68	90	42
Lightheadedness/ dizziness	87	78	78	95	98
Abdominal pain	46			75	23
Mental clouding	77	28		93	25
Facial flushing/ sweating	77			72	18
Visual abnormalities	69				17
Problems sleeping	46			84	54
Breathing difficulty	64			85	37
Memory difficulty	54			93	
Fainting	54	61			69
Tremulousness	49	38		58	17
Chest pain		24		78	32

1. Deb, A., Morgenshtern, K., et al. A survey-based analysis of symptoms in patients with postural orthostatic tachycardia syndrome. *Baylor University Medical Center Proceedings* 2015;28(2):157-159

2. Thieben, M.J., Sandroni, P., et al. Postural orthostatic tachycardia syndrome: the mayo clinic experience. *Mayo Clinic Proceedings* 2007;82(3):308-313

3. Heyer, G. L., Fedak, E. M., et al. Symptoms predictive of postural tachycardia syndrome (POTS) in the adolescent headache patient. *Headache* 2013;53:947-953

4. MyHeart.net/pots-syndrome/ 2015

5. Parsalk, A.K., Singer, W., et al. Orthostatic intolerance without postural tachycardia: how much dysautonomia? *Clinical Autonomia Research.* 2013;23(4):181-188

The most frequent symptoms reported by POTS patients were: palpitations, fatigue, headache, lightheadedness/dizziness, difficulty concentrating and fainting.

What Secret Skin Clues Suggest POTS?

There are subtle skin signs, frequently overlooked, that are important clues to the presence of POTS. The most consistent and highly suggestive diagnostic physical sign of POTS are observed in the lower extremities. Associated with the excessive pooling of venous blood in the lower extremities is a bluish-purple discoloration of the legs below the knees that can be seen after standing for a few minutes. This clue goes by the name of acrocyanosis (extremity blueness). This bluish-purple pooling discoloration in the lower legs is usually generalized (whole legs), symmetrical (same pattern on both legs) and bilateral (both legs). But, it can also be blotchy and spotty. Congestion (over filling of venous blood) within the veins causes the lower legs to turn blue and feel cool and moist to touch. When the venous stretching has been chronic, swelling of the feet can occur. POTS patients do not report experiencing this bluish-purple discoloration clue of their legs. However, when looked for, these diagnostic clues – cool, moist and bluish-purple discoloration of both lower legs after standing can often be discovered.

Additional skin symptoms provide evidence of autonomic nervous system dysfunction in POTS patients. POTS patients frequently report experiencing facial paleness, facial or neck flushing and sweating of the neck, upper chest and arms. At times the flushing can be more generalized. Others report "Raynaud's phenomenon," a condition where the tips of fingers turn white with associated pain when exposed to the cold. Generally this paleness clears when the hands are warmed. Many observe itching and hives, but rarely report these to their health care provider. The presence of flushing, itching and/or hives suggests that mast cell activation may be complicating the POTS picture. These latter clues can occur in many other medical disorders, but are not as diagnostic of POTS as is the cool, moist, bluish-purple pooling discoloration clue in the lower legs.

Combining slowed movement of venous blood within the veins (diminished oxygen causes bluish blood) with intense sympathetic activity of skin vessels (attempting to constrict veins) leads to tachycardia and the cool, moist, bluish-purple pooling discoloration of the lower legs. Excessive sympathetic activity can induce mast cell activation with resultant flushing, itching and/or hives (See **Mast Cell Activation Disorder in Chapter 10**).

Chapter 8 describes **How to Test for POTS**

CHAPTER 8:

How to Test for POTS?

Evaluation of patients for possible POTS includes a detailed history of the onset of current symptoms, preceding events, triggers and progression. Information is necessary regarding background physical exercise, sleeping, eating and drug use patterns. Past history is also important. Unfortunately, no POTS specific blood tests are available to confirm the diagnosis.

All patients require a comprehensive medical examination focused on the cardiovascular systems, including examination of heart size, regularity of rhythm, murmurs, lungs, arteries and veins. In addition, detailed examination is required of the neurological, psychological, endocrine, musculoskeletal and gastrointestinal systems. A medical evaluation is a necessity, not only to confirm the POTS diagnosis, but also to rule out other explanations for one's symptoms.

During the physical examination, special attention is placed on examination of the skin, joint looseness and pain point locations. The abdomen is examined for tenderness and organ enlargement. The hands are examined for altered temperature, discoloration and dampness. The lower extremities are examined for coldness, bluish discoloration (venous pooling) and dampness while standing.

Routine Diagnostic Work-up

Complete Medical History

Diet and Exercise History

Physical Examination

Blood Tests

Electrocardiogram & 24 Hour Holter Monitor

Specialized Tests For POTS Include:

Head-Up-Tilt Test (HUTT) or Tilt Table Test (TTT)

While lying flat for 10 minutes, pulse and blood pressure are measured every minute. Then measured for an additional 10 minutes while a special table is gradually raised upright to a tilt of 70° (head end-up). Patients are strapped onto the tilt table to prevent the feet from supporting the upright body. Thus during tilting, the leg muscles cannot squeeze the veins and venous pooling will be maximized.

POTS has been defined by an increase in heart rate of greater than 40 bpm (beats per minute) in teenagers and adolescents (ages 12-19) or a rise greater than 30 bpm in adults or pulse rise equal to or greater than 120 bpm with a negligible fall in blood pressure during a gradual passive tilt (without weight-bearing). The HUTT has been the "Gold Standard" (most reliable) test for diagnosing POTS for years. (**Figure 6**).

Figure 6

Head-Up-Tilt Test (HUTT)

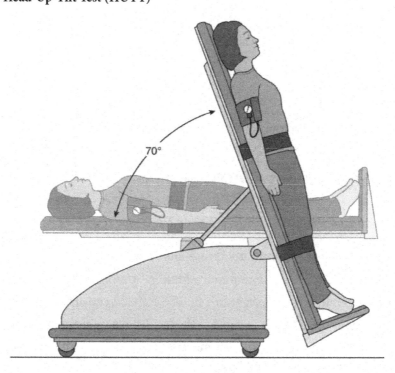

Ideally, the test is best performed in the morning and mid menstrual cycle in females, when it is most reliable. In fact, it has been determined that a HUTT performed in the morning can be positive for POTS, but when performed in the afternoon on the same individual, the HUTT could be normal.

Table 10: Typical HUTT Results from a POTS Patient

	Heart Rate beats/minute	Blood Pressure	Stroke Volume cc/beat	Cardiac Output cc/minute
Lying flat	72	120/80	75	5400 cc/min
Head-up 2 minutes	80	118/78	55 [↓27%]	4400 cc/min
Head-up 5 minutes	120	122/82	42 [↓44%]	5040 cc/min
Head-up 10 minutes	145			

As shown in **Table 10**, during standing for 2 minutes, orthostasis (ability to maintain function while upright) is stressed and both *stroke volume* and *cardiac output* (heart beats/minute X *stroke volume* cc/beat) fall significantly. In this example, all goes well because the autonomic nervous system response kicks-in at approximately 5 minutes and speeds up the heart rate to make up for the fall in *cardiac output*. Thus, tachycardia attempts to improve that all important *cardiac output* (120 X 42) to 5,040 cc/minute and partially corrects and restores *cardiac output* and maintains brain blood flow. Note - the heart rate has speeded up from 72 to 120 beats/minute within 5 minutes of standing (tachycardia).

> *As simple as the results should be for interpretation of the presence or absence of POTS, not even specialists performing the test know how to properly interpret the results. Over 18 months, Sara aged 23, experienced dizziness, flushing of her face, blurred vision and headaches immediately upon standing up and getting out of bed in the morning. When her symptoms became more frequent, the possibility of POTS was raised and the Tilt Table Test shown above was performed.*
>
> *A cardiologist performed this Tilt Table Test for Sara. Two cardiologists reviewed the test results, but misinterpreted*

*the results. Both were looking for a fall in blood pressure to
explain her dizziness and visual difficulties when upright
even though (a fall in blood pressure when upright is not
part of POTS). Because, there was no fall in blood pressure
at 70 degree tilt, they read the test as negative for orthostatic
hypotension (low blood pressure). That part was correct; she
did not have low blood pressure. But, they misinterpreted
the test results as negative for POTS, when the results
were 100% diagnostic for POTS. These cardiologists had
overlooked the fact that her supine (lying) pulse rate was 72
and it rose to 145 when tilted (a 69 beat rise) and (a rise to
greater than 120 beats/minute).*

*Even though her test results satisfied both requirements for
a diagnosis of POTS: tilted pulse rate rise (1) greater than
30 beats/min and (2) rate exceeded 120 beats/minute, these
cardiologists reported the test as negative for POTS. They
overlooked the significant tachycardia without a fall in blood
pressure response to assuming the upright posture - the most
reliable diagnostic predictor for POTS. Thus, they prevented
Sara from getting the correct diagnosis and treatment she
desperately needed.*

Head-Up Test (HUT) or Standing Test (ST)

In the HUT, pulse and blood pressure are measured while lying flat for 10
minutes and then every minute for an additional 10 minutes while standing
upright (like standing at attention without moving one's feet). This active
postural challenge (with weight-bearing) utilizes the same diagnostic criteria as for the HUTT. The HUT or ST is easier to perform because it does
not require the use of a specialized tilt table. Any healthcare provider can
conduct this test, as the **HUT requires no specialized equipmen**t – only

counting the pulse and measuring blood pressure if available to confirm the lack of BP fall (see **Table 10**).

POTS is still defined by an increase in heart rate of greater than 40 bpm (beats per minute) in teenagers and adolescents (ages 12-19) or a rise greater than 30 bpm in adults or pulse rise equal to or greater than 120 bpm with a negligible fall in blood pressure during 10 minutes of standing.

While HUTT remains the "Gold Standard" test for diagnosing POTS, the HUT remains a useful diagnostic tool for all medical personnel. Remember, similar to the HUTT, performance of the HUT is most reliable when performed in the morning rather than the afternoon, and be careful not to get hurt in case you fall.

Easy Screening Head-Up Test (E-HUT)

In the Easy Screening Head-Up Test only the pulse is measured while lying flat and standing for 10 minutes (**Table 11**). Check the pulse rate every two minutes both while lying down and while standing upright (like standing at attention without moving one's feet). An increase in heart rate of greater than 40 bpm (beats per minute) in teenagers and adolescents (ages 12-19) or rise greater than 30 bpm in adults or pulse greater than 120 bpm when standing suggests the presence of POTS. If the pulse rate rise is significant, share these results with your healthcare provider. This postural challenge can be a useful self-screening test for POTS. Remember, similar to the HUTT, performance of the Easy Screening Head-Up Test is most reliable when performed in the morning rather than the afternoon, and be careful not to get hurt in case you fall.

Table 11: Easy Screening Head-Up Test

Time	Supine (Lying Down) Pulse Rate	Standing Pulse Rate	POTS Associated Symptoms ??
Base-Line			
2 Minutes			
4 Minutes			
6 Minutes			
8 Minutes			
10 Minutes			
	Lowest Supine Reading	Highest Standing Reading	
	Maximal Pulse Rise (Change)		

Norepinephrine Blood Levels

To perform this test, norepinephrine (adrenaline) blood levels are obtained while supine (lying flat) and following standing for 10-15 minutes. Then the two results are compared. Among POTS patients, norepinephrine blood levels may be slightly elevated when supine. However, norepinephrine blood levels rise significantly post standing to levels much greater that normally measured when supine. (**Table 12**)

Table 12: Typical Results from A POTS Patient

Characteristics	Supine	Standing
Heart Rate (beats/minute)	72	122
Systolic Blood Pressure (mm Hg)	110	115
Norepinephrine blood level (ng/mL)	250	850

24 Hour Urinary Sodium Content

The quantities of salt and water within the body are watched very tightly. POTS patients generally have reduced quantities of both body water (hypovolemia) and reduced body salt. Salt (sodium) plays an important role within the blood to maintain osmotic pressure and prevent loss of fluid into the surrounding tissues. To maintain homeostasis (internal balance), the kidneys are in charge of conserving as much water and salt as necessary.

The low concentration of urinary sodium observed among those with POTS can be an indirect measurement of reduced salt intake and blood volume (dehydration and hypovolemia). A 24-hour urine containing less than 100 meq of sodium confirms low blood volume and conservation of salt by the body. POTS patients tend to have concentrated urine (dehydration promotes conservation of fluids by the kidneys). The goal of therapy of POTS is to have large quantities of dilute colorless urine as this confirms adequate intake of both liquids and salt.

Impedance Cardiography

Primarily a research instrument, impedance cardiography measures cardiac output (volume of blood pumped out by the heart per minute). When performed during a HUTT test, it can measure the amount of blood pumped out while supine and the reduction in output upon assuming the upright posture. Among POTS individuals the fall in cardiac output as the table tilts the head upward is much greater than that observed among individuals without POTS. Many POTS individuals experience signs or symptoms of altered brain function like dizziness, headache and visual disturbances when tilted upright. An abnormal impedance cardiogram test coexisting with onset of POTS symptoms when upright, can provide valuable confirmation of the relationship between cardiac output, brain blood flow and POTS symptoms.

Echocardiography

Echocardiograms (sonograms of the heart utilizing sound waves) can measure the percentage of blood forced out from the heart with each beat. That percentage is called the Ejection Fraction (EF). The normal EF is 55-70% for healthy individuals. It is utilized to rule out structural cardiac abnormalities. Echocardiography can also evaluate the structure and function of the heart valves and muscle segments. Other than a reduced EF when upright, echocardiograms performed among POTS patients are usually normal.

Trans-Cranial Ultrasound

Trans-Cranial Ultrasound is primarily a research instrument utilized to approximate cerebral blood flow. Ultrasound utilizes sound waves to measure blood flow within a major artery of the brain – this approximates cerebral blood flow. Ultrasound was originally developed by the navy to detect motion of submarines deep under water. Among POTS patients, it can be utilized to demonstrate the reduction in cerebral blood flow associated with assuming the upright posture.

Valsalva Maneuver Test (VMT)

The Valsalva maneuver is a test of the circulatory system's response to "straining" (bearing down), like when having a bowel movement. Heavy weight lifting, blowing a wind or brass musical instrument and coughing are also examples of "straining." Valsalva testing is performed by blowing hard against resistance in a standardized way and is considered as a research tool.

Early in the straining process, pressure within the inner chest is increased, placing increased pressure on the major veins entering the chest carrying blood back to the heart. This increased pressure within the chest reduces the blood from returning back to the heart, resulting in a prompt reduction in cardiac filling, cardiac output and blood pressure. Because the volume of blood returning back to the heart among POTS patients is already reduced, straining results in an early exaggerated decrease in blood pressure and cerebral blood flow. Similar to those changes during standing, excessive blood accumulates within the abdomen, pelvis-thighs and legs.

Later, following release of the straining in individuals without POTS, venous blood rushes into the heart resulting in a rapid recovery of the blood pressure to the original level followed by a temporary "overshoot" to higher pulse and blood pressure levels.

Among POTS patients, this post-straining cardiac refilling process consists of an even greater volume of blood. Therefore, both the heart rate and blood pressure demonstrate an "overshoot," with a much higher rise following discontinuation of the Valsalva maneuver. Baroreceptors turned on during the early fall in blood pressure stimulate this out-pouring of norepinephrine contributing to the greater tachycardia and larger blood pressure "overshoot."

Reduced brain perfusion associated with the early straining phase of the Valsalva maneuver can also trigger POTS symptoms – dizziness, headache, lightheadedness, visual disturbances, abdominal pain etc. During the "overshoot" phase, headaches are common.

Quantitative Sudomotor Axon Reflex Test (QSART)

The quantitative sudomotor axon reflex test is a research test for dysautonomia. It assesses sympathetic nerve fibers (sweat function). The test may reveal patchy or generalized loss of sweating in arms and legs (specific dysautonomia). This abnormality is believed to be caused by injury of the autonomic nerves of the skin by antibodies associated with an infection. Some POTS patients demonstrate localized areas with loss of sweating function.

Chapter 9 provides **My POWER over POTS Plan**

My POWER over POTS Plan

What Do I Need To Know? How Can I Take Back My LIFE?

Learning about POTS, its causes, symptoms, physiological mechanisms, diagnostic tests and treatments are essential if one wants to manage the poor adaptation of the cardiovascular, nervous and muscular systems and eventually overcome the disturbing manifestations of this syndrome. Understanding the contents of this book will help you select a knowledgeable and experienced physician to guide you through your rehabilitation and recovery program.

Generally, most adolescent POTS patients experience gradual improvement over the course of several years. "Mother Nature" and "Father Time," among the "Best Doctors," help your autonomic nervous system mature and overcome the challenges of your newly acquired taller structure. Other adults struggle with symptoms for many years.

Rather than a specific disease, individuals with POTS experience a collection of multiple alterations in the normal physiological mechanisms that contribute to an assortment of symptoms. While most patients with POTS would like to find a magic pill that will correct the condition, treatment is more complicated than that. Whereas multiple functioning physiologic processes are required to maintain normal cardiac filling by return flow of blood from the lower body, treatment likewise requires a more complex therapeutic approach.

Each patient exhibits a variable combination of abnormalities of blood volume, salt intake, venous efficacy, sleep and breathing patterns, muscular and cardiac atrophy due to deconditioning. Each case is different and unique. Therefore, each patient will require a customized rehabilitation program designed to correct those abnormalities most troubling to her or him.

Efficient movement of blood from the lower body back to the heart for recirculation to the whole body requires that all physiologic processes work together in harmony. The goal of treatment for reversing the incapacitating and disturbing symptoms of POTS is encouragement of return of normal physiologic function to all components.

POTS recovery goals should be both realistic and promote progression to heath. You too, can improve your cardiovascular, nervous and muscular systems and overcome the disturbing symptoms of POTS. You too, can improve. You too, can gain **POWER over POTS!**

What Are the Keys To POWER over POTS?

The keys to POTS recovery are learning how to avoid and overcome triggers, correcting low blood volume by increasing salt and fluid intake and reversing cardiovascular and lower extremity muscular deconditioning by establishing a strengthening and endurance exercise training program.

Keeping records is an essential component of a **POWER over POTS** rehabilitation program. Consider utilizing the Recovery Records provided in this book to monitor your progress. Utilize these recovery tools to become empowered instead of remaining powerless.

How Do I Avoid Triggers (Precipitating, Aggravating Factors)?

First and most important is learning how avoid triggers, precipitating and aggravating factors. Where possible, avoid prolonged lying down, prolonged standing especially in a fixed position without leg movement and standing-up quickly. Avoid those actions that encourage pooling of blood into the lower body. Even prolonged bed rest and exercising against resistance like weight lifting can promote pooling of blood. Before standing up, try sitting and pretend to dance on the floor with your feet - thus encouraging venous return of blood to the heart.

When required to stand up for an extended period of time, keep moving your legs, shifting your weight from foot to foot and contracting your thighs and buttocks muscles, thus encouraging venous return to the heart.

Avoid hot weather, excessive heat, dehydration and hot tubs. Even activities like hot showers may worsen dehydration and accentuate physical fatigue. Minimize heavy meals that encourage excessive movement of fluids from the bloodstream into the intestinal tract to aid in digestion, adding to reduction of circulating blood volume and making symptoms worse.

Having POTS is synonymous with chronic stress, and stress only encourages worsening of symptoms. Lack of sleep plays an important role in furthering fatigue.

Some patients experience worsening of symptoms when going up in an elevator or while flying in airplanes. Both activities encourage gravitational shifting of blood towards the feet. When flying, plan to do calf muscle exercises, stand up regularly, and walk up and down the aisles. If sitting in a cramped airplane seat presents a problem, uncross legs (crossing legs obstructs venous return), repeatedly move your legs and feet (alternate toes up and down), squirm around in your seat, all encourage venous return to the heart.

Additional triggers include physical fatigue, lack of sleep, excessive stress and illicit drugs. Excessive caffeine and more potent diuretics that increase urination and reduce blood volume may aggravate POTS symptoms. Menses especially tend to accentuate symptoms.

Many daily activities can precipitate or aggravate POTS symptoms by encouraging dehydration, venous pooling and physical deconditioning. **Table 13** provides triggers that worsen your symptoms and steps you can take to avoid them.

Table 13: Count the Ways to Encourage Venous Return to the Heart

Where possible, avoid these triggers:	Instead try:
Prolonged sitting and lying down	Force yourself to be upright and active (exercise)
Sitting in a cramped seat like an airplane	Uncross legs (crossing legs inhibits venous return), repeatedly move your legs and feet (alternate toes up and down), squirm around in your seat. Get up regularly and walk up and down the aisles.
Prolonged standing especially in a fixed position without leg movement	Keep moving your legs, shifting your weight from foot to foot, toes to heels
Standing-up quickly	Before standing-up, try sitting and pretend to dance on the floor with your feet, then stand up gradually
Hot weather, showers, tubs and excessive heat	Choose comfortable temperatures, avoid heat
Prolonged bed rest	Force yourself to be upright and active (exercise)
Heavy meals	Eat light meals
Exercising against resistance	Exercise your legs, thighs and buttocks muscles
Dehydration	Increase fluid and salt intake

POWER over POTS keys to recovery are learning how to:

- Avoid and overcome triggers

- Increase fluid intake

- Increase salt intake

- Reverse cardiovascular muscular deconditioning

- Reverse lower extremity muscular deconditioning

- Establish a strengthening and endurance exercise training program.

- Obtain adequate quality sleep

- Reduce stress

Keeping Recovery Records is an essential component of a Recovery Program. Consider utilizing the Recovery Records like these provided to set goals and monitor your progress. A plan without a goal is just a wish.

———————

The keys to POTS recovery are learning how to avoid and overcome triggers, correcting low blood volume by increasing salt and fluid intake and reversing cardiovascular and lower extremity muscular deconditioning by establishing a strengthening and endurance exercise training program.

———————

How Do I Maintain Adequate Blood Volume?

How Do I Increase My Fluid Intake?

Most adolescents and adults do not consume an adequate daily intake of fluids and many have low blood volume. Dehydration results in hypovolemia (reduced circulating blood volume). Hypovolemia results in reduced volume of blood returning to the heart. Patients with POTS need to increase their daily fluid intake significantly to expand their blood volume. This chart provides daily fluid intake guidelines for POTS patients to increase their daily fluid intake up to 2-3 quarts per day. For most patients 2-3 quarts daily are adequate. However, some will require 4 quarts per day. See Recommended Daily Fluid Intake for POTS Patients in **Table 14.**

Table 14:

Recommended Daily Fluid Intake for POTS Patients			
Liters	Quarts	8 ounce Cups	Ounces
2	2	8	60
3	3	12	90
4	4	16	120

(Quantities are rounded off to simplify the chart)

How Do I Monitor My Progress?

Increased water intake is useful, but non-caffeinated high salt fluids are preferable like soups, tomato-based juices and "sports drinks." Utilize cups or ounces for measuring daily intake, whichever is easier for you.

I KNOW HOW TO MANAGE POTS
INCREASING FLUID INTAKE IS IMPORTANT FOR ME

	M	T	W	T	F	S	S
AM							
LUNCH							
PM							
DINNER							
EVENING							
TOTALS							

Goal

DAILY/WEEKLY

TOTAL

INCREASED FLUID INTAKE
IS KEY TO FEELING BETTER

You can utilize Recovery Records similar to this one to set goals for adequate fluid intake. As you become more familiar with the process of setting and meeting your **Daily Fluid Intake Goals**, you can move up to setting **Weekly Fluid Intake Goals**.

Step 1: Set Daily Fluid Intake Goals,

When comfortable move to step 2

Step 2: Set Weekly Fluid Intake Goals

How Do I Increase My Salt Intake?

Adequate salt (sodium chloride) is required within the circulating blood to maintain osmotic pressure within the blood vessels. Osmotic pressure regulates the flow of liquids between the bloodstream and the tissues of the body. Reduced salt intake leads to reduced osmotic pressure of the blood and leakage of fluid out of blood vessels and into the spaces between cells, especially the lower limbs. Fluids move from reduced osmotic pressure within the blood vessels toward the tissues with higher osmotic pressure. Thus, salt or sodium plays an important role in maintaining blood osmotic pressure and volume, and encourages venous return of blood to the heart.

Patients with POTS generally require a significant increase in sodium intake to increase the osmotic pressure within the blood vessels. The words "sodium" and "salt" are often used interchangeably, but they are different. Salt consists of 40% sodium and 60% chloride. Ideally, healthy adults should limit sodium intake to less than 2,400 mg per day. The average adult intake of sodium is approximately 3,300 mg per day. However, POTS patients require greater daily salt intake, usually 6,000-10,000 mg of sodium (6-10 Gm) per day.

"Sports-drinks" contain approximately 100 mg of sodium and 250 calories of sugar per 8 ounces and are pleasant tasting. Many POTS patients depend on "sports-drinks" to increase their salt and fluid intake. If calorie restriction is important, lower calorie "sports-drinks" are available. While "sports-drinks" are able to increase both liquid volume and salt simultaneously, the daily intake of these drinks needs to be increased substantially to meet the needs of POTS patients.

Pleasant tasting commercial rehydration salt sticks and powders are also available that can be easily dissolved in drinking water to increase daily sodium intake. They can contain from 200 to 800 mg of sodium.

The majority of sodium in the daily American diet comes from processed and prepared foods. Adding salt to food and eating foods high in sodium is encouraged. High sodium foods include breads, cured meats, cheeses, pickled foods, canned vegetables, frozen dinners, salted nuts and snack foods, tomato based sauces, soy sauce, restaurant food, broths and soups. A one gram sodium chloride tablet (only 1/3 is sodium) can be added to one's daily intake, but taking many tablets may result in abdominal discomfort, even nausea.

Individuals with healthy kidneys normally rapidly excrete salt into the urine after it's eaten. A 24-hour urinary sodium test can provide useful information regarding the adequacy or inadequacy of sodium intake. Low urinary sodium, as seen in most POTS patients, implies reduced intake and maximal saving of sodium by the body.

Learn to read food labels for the sodium content in mg. POTS patients require greater daily salt intake, usually 6,000-10,000 mg of sodium (6-10 Gm) per day. Learn to generously add salt to many of your daily foods. (1 teaspoon of salt = 5 Gm salt = 2,400 mg sodium).

Why Is Increasing Salt Intake Easy For Teens?

Since most teenagers' favorite foods are high in sodium, this is usually the easiest change to make. Most snacks, fast foods and restaurant items like nachos, soups, cheeseburgers and cheesy casseroles are notoriously high in sodium. So, having to increase sodium can sound like a dream come true. Unfortunately, many of these items that are high in sodium may also be high in fat. If weight gain is a concern for you, there are many ways to increase sodium content and still be mindful of high fat and high calorie foods.

What Are The Best High Sodium Foods To Eat?

- Lean deli meats that are high in sodium like corned beef, pastrami, turkey and roast beef. Avoid the meats that are higher in fat such as bologna, salami, prosciutto and ham.
- Store bought rotisserie chicken
- Low fat fish options such as smoked salmon (lox), herring, tuna and sardines
- Canned soups that aren't cream based
- Canned beans including beans, baked beans and chili
- Tofu
- Cooked lean chicken or tofu with soy sauce, teriyaki sauce, fish sauce, pasta sauce, buffalo wing sauce
- Packaged Asian noodle soup (add protein by making an egg drop like soup by mixing in a raw egg into the soup while it cooks)
- Packaged vegetable, chicken and beef broth
- Smoked and salted almonds and other nuts
- Low fat cheeses
- Canned vegetables not in a cream sauce
- Pickles and olives (some kids like eating frozen pickle juice cubes made by freezing pickle juice in ice cube trays)
- Packaged macaroni and cheese (add a defrosted package of mashed frozen butternut squash to the sauce to lower the calories per serving)
- Sauerkraut (add sauerkraut to a low fat or vegetarian hot dog)
- Breakfast cereals
- Canned vegetable juice
- Low calorie or light sports beverages

How Do I Select Foods High In Sodium?

Increase your daily salt intake - select foods high in sodium. Select from the following high sodium foods: Each numbered circle represents 100s of mgs of sodium, e.g. (⑧ = 800 mg of sodium, ⑮ = 1500 mg of sodium). [All measures are approximations]

Table 15: Selecting Foods High in Sodium

Selecting Foods High in Sodium
Each numbered circle = 100s of mgs of Sodium [approximates]

restaurant dinners	⑱	deli pastrami, turkey	⑥
cured, smoked meats and fish	⑮	tomato juice, vegetable cocktail (1 cup)	⑥
potato salad (1 cup)	⑬	spaghetti sauce (½ cup), mashed potato (1 cup)	⑥
salt (1/2 tsp)	⑫	luncheon meats (2 slices), hamburger (1)	⑤
frozen dinners	⑪	pizza, cheese meat topping (1 slice)	④
broths, soups, baked beans and chili (1 cup)	⑩	tomato based sauces (1/4 cup)	④
potato au gratin	⑩	Italian sauce (1/2 cup),	④
soy sauce (1 Tbs)	⑨	canned vegetables (1/2 cup)	④
tuna salad (1 cup), sandwich burger (1)	⑧	pepperoni, salami (5 slices), bacon (3 slices)	④
cheese-burger, grilled chicken sandwich (1)	⑧	cheese (2 slices), cottage cheese (1/2 cup)	④
canned soups (1 can)	⑧	biscuit, bagel, croissant (1), pancake(2)	④
dill pickle (1), pretzels hard salted (10)	⑧	chili and cocktail sauce (2 Tbs)	④
instant noodle soup (packet)	⑧	apple, cherry pie (1 slice)	③
hot dog, smoked sausage, ham slice	⑦	salad dressings (2 Tbs)	③

Use this information to familiarize yourself with your salt intake. Learn how to measure your starting daily food and drink sodium intake. Only then, can you take steps to significantly increase your daily and weekly sodium intake.

How Do I Monitor My Progress?

Once familiar with Salt Intake Tracking, utilize this simple Recovery Record that allows you to record only the approximate 100s of mgs of sodium ingested. This Recovery Record makes it easier to track daily goals and sodium intake.

In the sample provided, breakfast consisted of:

1 bagel = ④

2 slices of cheese = ④

1 glass of milk = ①

Total breakfast = 900 mg of sodium

The **Daily Goal** in this example is **6,000 mg of sodium (3 X 20)**

SAMPLE
I KNOW HOW TO MANAGE POTS
INCREASING SALT INTAKE IS IMPORTANT FOR ME

Daily Salt Tracker [Month] _____ [Day] _____

AM	④④①
LUNCH	
PM	SAMPLE
DINNER	
EVENING	
TOTALS	
	①②③④ ⑦ ⑨ ⑩⑪ ⑫⑬⑭⑮⑯⑰⑱⑲⑳

Goal

⑳⑳⑳

DAILY

TOTAL

INCREASED SODIUM INTAKE IS
KEY TO FEELING BETTER

I KNOW HOW TO MANAGE POTS
INCREASING SALT INTAKE IS IMPORTANT FOR ME

Daily Salt Tracker [Month] _____ [Day] _____

AM	
LUNCH	
PM	
DINNER	
EVENING	
TOTALS	
	①②③④⑤⑥⑦⑧⑨⑩⑪⑫⑬⑭⑮⑯⑰⑱⑲⑳

Goal

DAILY

TOTAL

INCREASED SODIUM INTAKE IS
KEY TO FEELING BETTER

Why Are We So Out-of-Shape?

Most POTS patients start out with poor exercise tolerance. They complain of rapid heart rate and early fatigue when attempting exercise and are unable to participate in strenuous activity. Physical deconditioning plays a major role in contributing to the chronic fatigue associated with POTS. Physical deconditioning is similar to that seen in healthy individuals after prolonged periods of bed rest while recovering from a major illness and plays a major role in contributing to this chronic fatigue associated with POTS.

Because patients with POTS do not tolerate being upright, they tend to avoid physical exercise and suffer because of their physical deconditioning. Prolonged physical inactivity encourages cardiac deconditioning and atrophy (loss of muscle) with a decrease in the volume of blood pumped with each beat - also diminishing physical endurance. A structured muscular strengthening and endurance exercise program will help you reverse cardiovascular and muscular deconditioning and acquire **POWER over POTS!**

How Do I Get In Shape?

How Do I Achieve Muscular Strengthening and Cardiovascular Endurance?

Being out of condition demands that rehabilitation begins with small activities and only then increased gradually. Gradually increasing exercise by strengthening thigh and leg muscles and enhancing venous return from the lower extremities is an essential component of any rehabilitation program. Muscular pumping during exercise, massages blood up the thighs and legs via the veins, contributing to the return of blood back to the heart. Multiple activities are available to strengthen the lower body muscular pumps and encourage venous return back to the heart. Multiple opportunities are available each day to find time to overcome venous pooling in the legs. Starting with light intensity activities like getting up and strolling around for a few minutes is better than nothing. Even just lifting weights with the legs will be beneficial.

What Exercise Is Best For Me?

Recumbent cycling, rowing machines and swimming are the best tolerated and preferred starting exercises. These activities encourage exercising that avoids upright exercising. Gradually increase time spent exercising and/or the intensity of the exercise. Start out with 5, 10 or 15 minutes of exercise 2-3 days per week - whatever you can tolerate. If only one or two minutes is all you can tolerate, that's fine. Everyone usually begins at a very low starting point. Save upright exercising until able to perform the recumbent exercises for at least 20 minutes 2-3 times per week. Then add endurance exercise training including walking, dancing, stationary cycling, tread-mill walking, elliptical trainers, jogging, and aerobics. Squats with the back against the wall and lifting weights with the legs are also beneficial. Gradually increase the weekly quantity. Aim for an ultimate goal of 30-60 minutes per day, 5-6 days per week.

Establish an individualized progressive leg-based exercise training pro-gram. Select those exercises you consider best, based on available equipment and your likings. **SCHEDULE TIME INTO YOUR DAILY SCHEDULE FOR THAT EXERCISE AND COMMIT TO DO IT**. Select an exercise or preferably a combination of exercises, set a weekly minutes goal and record your progress. With each week, gradually increase your exercise minutes goal. Some POTS specialists believe that exercise is the most crit-ical component of any recovery program. Exercise training can dramati-cally improve symptoms of POTS and each step of improvement convinces sufferers that **POWER over POTS** is possible. **POTS CAN BE BEAT!**

Why Is Starting An Exercise Program So Difficult?

Behavior change, especially exercising, is difficult for most people. Starting an exercise program can be really difficult, especially when you feel horri-ble. Initiating an exercise program in a teen or adult who doesn't feel well, can be even more challenging. While exercise is a critical component to recovery from POTS, compliance with an exercise program is usually the hardest aspect of the teen's or adult's Recovery Program. To increase the likelihood of your teenager beginning the exercise program, consider these helpful options.

If it weren't really, really important, everyone could just let you lie in bed and rest. But, if you want to take back your life, you are the only one who can fight this battle. Unfortunately, exercise is one thing no one else can do for you. So just decide how you are going to do it.

Getting started is the hardest part. Sometimes, having a scheduled appointment with a professional encourages positive progress. Some investigators believe endurance training is the most important therapeutic way to go. Exercise expands blood volume, increases heart strength, stroke volume and cardiac output and improves postural intolerance. Once you feel better, remember to keep up your exercise program – otherwise, what you don't use you will lose again.

Use it ...Regain it ...Retain POWER over POTS!

Tips for How I Can Get Started

Here are some tips other teens with POTS utilized to get motivated when exercise was the last thing they wanted to do. These can increase the likelihood for success.

- Start off really slowly. If you do too much the first day, you may be really exhausted the next day and then use your exhaustion as an excuse not to exercise again. Beware...it's a trap. Start slow, add a little more at a time, and work up gradually. You might start with just a minute or two a day for the first week. That's okay. The goal is to increase your exercise gradually, so that you regain your strength. Increase the duration and intensity as slowly and gradually as you need to. The important thing is that you...Do Some Exercise Every Day.

- Try and get a friend or relative to join you. Maybe you can start with a short exercise with a friend. Maybe a friend can keep you company while you do your exercises. Having a workout partner helps you stick to a plan.

- Schedule a regular time each day and stick to it. The more you can build a routine into your schedule, the more likely you are to stick with your program.

- If possible, you can try and work out with a trainer or physical therapist that is knowledgeable about exercise and POTS. However, if this option is not available to you, don't use it as an excuse for not doing your exercises. Your exercise is your responsibility. Exercise is your ticket to **POWER over POTS.**

How Do I Monitor My Progress?

Use these Recovery Records to design your individualized exercise strengthening and conditioning program. Select an exercise or preferably a combination of exercises, set a weekly goal in minutes and record your progress. With each week, gradually add more minutes to your exercise goal. Exercise training can dramatically improve your POTS symptoms and each improvement step will convince you that **POTS Can Be Beat.**

I KNOW HOW TO MANAGE POTS
INCREASING EXERCISE IS IMPORTANT FOR ME

	M	T	W	T	F	S	S
AM							
LUNCH							
PM							
DINNER							
EVENING							
TOTALS							

BECOMING MORE ACTIVE IS
THE BEST MEDICINE FOR ME

GOAL

WEEKLY

TOTAL

Recumbent cycling, rowing machines
and swimming are the best tolerated
and preferred starting exercises.
These activities encourage exercising
that avoids upright exercising.

Are There Useful Tips for Overcoming Venous Pooling?

Multiple opportunities are available each day to overcome venous pooling in the legs. In addition to exercising, the following activities will strengthen your lower body muscular pumps and encourage venous return back to your heart. These exercises can be especially useful when sitting for prolonged periods of time or while flying.

The following activities strengthen the lower body muscular pumps and encourage venous return back to the heart.

Tips for Overcoming Venous Pooling

Useful Standing Activities to Consider:

- Walk instead of standing still

- Contract (tighten) the abdominal, buttock (fanny), thigh and calf muscles repeatedly

- Shift weight from one leg to the other

- Stand alternately on your toes and heels (rocking motion)

- Stand on one leg and bend the other

- Stand on tiptoes as high as you can (heel raises)

Useful Sitting Activities to Consider:

- Raise and lower knees up toward chest
- Dance with your feet on the floor
- Roll ankles (draw circles with toes)
- Raise your toes and heels (rocking motion) alternately
- Cross legs together at the ankles and repeatedly squeeze legs together
- Cross legs together at the ankles and repeatedly raise legs

Additional Useful Exercises to Consider:

- Leg presses, raises, step-ups and curls
- Abdominal crunches.
- Wall squats
- Jogging in a pool (use floatation belt)

Avoid prolonged crossing legs when sitting as it impedes lower leg venous flow. And always, while exercising, utilize your abdominal muscles and keep breathing. Avoid breath-holding while exercising.

What about Compression Stockings?

Under experimental conditions in adolescents, inflation of compression garments to the lower body has yielded positive results. Lower body compression squeezes the blood pooled in the lower body back towards the heart. Improvement in return of blood to the heart by lower body compression can reverse many of the POTS-related orthostatic symptoms.

For this reason, support hose have been recommended in the past to decrease the caliber of the veins of the legs and encourage venous return to the heart. However, we now know that support stockings are not rec-ommended as they are counter-productive. Using this artificial "crutch" only delays the physiologic improvement of weak muscles and prolongs the duration of the POTS symptoms. Furthermore, most females strongly object to wearing the thick, tight-pressure support hose.

Therefore, compression stockings have been reserved for those who have been resistant to the usual therapy. If utilized, the stockings need to be the custom fitted and provide built-in compression of 30-40 mm of Hg.

Do I Need Regenerative Regular Sleep?

Today, young people have excessive demands on their time - leaving pre-cious little time for sleep. Demands come from schooling, extracurricular activities and "screen activities" (socializing, gaming and entertainment). Only a small percentage of adolescents obtain adequate nightly sleep. Yet, the American Academy of Pediatrics recommends that 13-18 year olds obtain 8-10 hours of sleep nightly. Fatigue associated with lack of adequate sleep affects cognitive, emotional and physical functions. Sleep is essential, as many important metabolic bodily functions take place during sleep, like the manufacturing of our vital hormones. During sleep we make repairs, regain energy and rejuvenate our bodies and minds.

Sleep deprivation is common among adolescents. It's estimated that the majority of POTS patients report sleep disorders. POTS patients often report trouble falling asleep, unsatisfactory and unrefreshing sleep and excessive daytime sleepiness. In addition, they report poor sleep quality with frequent restlessness and awakenings during sleep. When awake, they report trouble staying awake, trouble concentrating and daytime tiredness. Without restorative sleep, one's tolerance for disturbing symptoms goes way down. Inadequate and poor quality sleep almost guarantees fatigue, feeling tired all the time and reduced quality of life.

Plan to complete your daily activities at a reasonable hour so as to permit at least 8 hours of restful sleep as often as possible. Avoid stimulants, distractions and strenuous exercise close to bedtime. While you may think you can pull an "all-nighter" and catch up and recharge your energy batteries by occasionally sleeping longer tomorrow, fatigue refuses to go away. Catching up on sleep is more of a dream than a reality.

Do I Need A Regular Meal Schedule?

Maintaining a regular meal schedule makes it much easier to plan and achieve your goals to increase salt and fluid intake. Many POTS patients depend on "sports-drinks" to increase their salt and fluid intake. "Sports-drinks" are easy to obtain and carry with you. Thus, they are a convenient way to increase both liquid volume and salt simultaneously.

Whereas, blood flow to the intestinal organs is increased following a heavy meal, it's best not to stand up suddenly following a heavy meal. Some POTS patients choose to lie down after eating to avoid the symptoms associated with this "brain steal" like dizziness, faintness, light-headedness and blurred vision. This phenomenon is similar to that seen among infants who regularly fall asleep after eating, when blood is purposely diverted to the digestive organs.

Can Some Medications Aggravate POTS Symptoms?

Both drugs that dilate blood vessels and diuretics that encourage excretion of fluid can worsen POTS symptoms and should be avoided. Some oral contraceptives contain drosperinone, a hormone that promotes low blood volume and they too should also be avoided.

Should I Completely Avoid Illegal Drugs and Alcohol?

Teenage years can be a time that teens decide to experiment with drugs and alcohol. While unhealthy and dangerous for all teenagers, these can be especially dangerous for individuals with POTS. Illegal drugs, alcohol and "energy drinks" greatly affect your body's autonomic system by hampering your body's ability to regulate itself. When these drugs and alcohol are combined with an already compromised autonomic system, the results can be disastrous.

Can Breathing Patterns Reduce My Anxiety, Stress & Hyperventilation?

It is common for teens with POTS who have never had prior mental health challenges to become suddenly anxious and/or depressed. But to be clear, the POTS symptoms are not a result of anxiety or depression. The POTS illness began first and the resultant anxiety and/or depression came from losing control over one's life due to the symptoms of POTS. Suffering with an undiagnosed, frustrating illness can stress-out even the strongest amongst us.

Dealing with the disturbing symptoms of POTS can result in high levels of anxiety. Emotional stress sets off involuntary brainstem signals that tighten one's muscles – all part of the preparation for battle reaction. Unfortunately, the diaphragm muscles (muscles normally utilized to move air in and out of the lungs) are included among these tightened muscles. A locked (tightened) diaphragm forces one to breath by utilizing the muscles of the rib cage to lift the ribs and allow movement of air into the lungs. Rapid chest breathing is not as efficient as calm abdominal breathing.. The normal breathing rate for adults sitting quietly averages 13 breaths per minute. Rapid breathing at rest is known as hyperventilation Twenty percent of people don't know it, but they always hyperventilate. Most people only become rapid chest breathers when stressed (stress-related hyperventilators)

Emotional stress can initiate rapid shallow chest breathing, dizziness and chest pains. Hyperventilation (rapid chest breathing) should be reserved for physical exercise and danger - not emotional stress. Hyperventilation is expected when running or fighting for one's life. Hyperventilation when physically inactive can have detrimental effects on body metabolism. Carbon dioxide is the most frequent by-product of body metabolism. Blowing off excessive carbon dioxide (faster than you can produce it) is called hypocapnia (low carbon dioxide blood level). This over-breathing and hypocapnia decreases red blood cell (hemoglobin's) oxygen carrying capacity, increases nerve and muscle irritability and can also promote arterial spasms.

Both hyperventilation (rapid shallow breathing) and hypocapnia (low carbon dioxide blood level) are frequently observed among POTS patients. Those who hyperventilate, regularly report "difficulty getting a deep breath," and being "unable to catch their breath." They frequently interrupt their speech with sighs and gasp for breath before speaking. When POTS patients blow off excessive CO_2, it causes major alterations in bodily functions and intensifies their POTS symptoms i.e., tachycardia, dizziness, faintness, numbness, weakness and chest pains, etc.

Tips for Learning Healthy Breathing

Breathing is an important link between your mind and your body. Slowing down your breathing can be a powerful tool for reducing your anxiety and stress. Learning healthy relaxing abdominal breathing can be an important component of gaining **POWER over POTS.**

For relaxed breathing air in

- Breath in effortlessly and slowly via your nose (aim for 4-7 breaths per minute)

- Practice moving the diaphragm down to expand your lungs

- Expand your abdomen like a balloon with inhalation (**BELLY OUT**)

For relaxed breathing air out

- Exhale slowly via the mouth saying "HAAAAH" to slow exhalation (**BELLY IN**)

- Squeeze in your abdominal muscles to raise the diaphragm up to force air out

- [While learning – push in on your abdomen to raise the diaphragm]

- Make exhalation take longer than the inhalation phase of breathing

For relaxed breathing

- Encourage abdominal motion rather than stressed upper chest breathing

- Monitor movement - place left hand on chest and right hand on abdomen

- Look for minimal chest and maximal abdominal expansion

- Relaxed slow breathing encourages healthy physiology and mental calm

- Aim to slow breathing to less than 7 breaths per minute

- Repeatedly practice relaxed slow abdominal breathing daily

Calm relaxed breathing is primarily abdominal, dependent on the diaphragm muscles to move air in and out of the lungs. Relaxed babies while sleeping can be seen using their diaphragmatic muscles to breath, making their abdomens rise (breathing in) and fall (breathing out). Unlike calm abdominal breathing, rapid chest breathing associated with stress puts strain on the joints of the rib cage resulting in characteristic rib cage pain. During the inspiratory (breathing air in) phase of breathing, increased negative pressure within the chest cavity encourages the return of blood to the heart. However, persistent over-breathing (hyperventilation) results in excessive exhaling of carbon dioxide (CO_2), abnormally lowering blood acidity.

The rib cage consists of 12 ribs on each side with 12 joints between the ends of the ribs and the cartilages that fill in the space between the ribs and the breast bones. An additional 12 joints are on each side where the cartilages join the breast bones. Thus, the rib cage consists of a total of 48 joints, 24 on each side. See **Figure** 7. The most common pain among POTS patients is rib cage pain, localized to these joints and associated with localized tenderness. Whereas many POTS patients are stressed out and hyperventilate, pain and tenderness in some of the joints of the rib cage are very common among POTS patients.

Figure 7: The Rib Cage and Its 48 Joints [not all are visible]

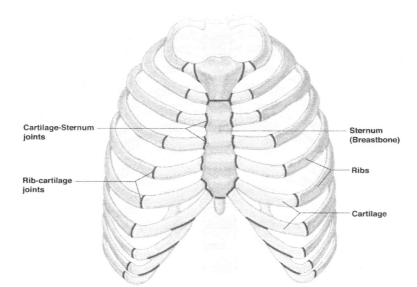

Can I Benefit From Psychological Support?

Experiencing a bizarre assortment of undiagnosed symptoms over a prolonged time period can emotionally stress out even the strongest of us.
You may appear to be physically healthy on the outside, but you have been
psychologically bruised. Disability-imposed restrictions on school, social
and work activities may have placed you at increased risk of depression.
Education and psychological counselling are important components of the
rehabilitation for many POTS patients and aid in recovery. If you feel the
need for help to tide you over this temporary bump in the road of life, ask
for help.

Breathing is an important link between
your mind and your body. Slowing down
your breathing can be a powerful tool
for reducing your anxiety and stress.
Learning healthy relaxing abdominal
breathing can be an important
component of gaining POWER over POTS.

What If I Become Pregnant?

Whereas POTS primarily affects women of childbearing age, pregnancy does occur frequently among women with preexisting POTS. Having POTS does not place restrictions on becoming pregnant or carrying the pregnancy to delivery. However, establishing that the unexplained symptoms are related to POTS only becomes more difficult. The symptoms of POTS may generally worsen during the first three months (first trimester) of a pregnancy, often making a woman acutely aware that "something is not right". During the first trimester, nausea and vomiting tends to be worse when pregnancy is combined with POTS. However, as the pregnancy progresses, blood and plasma volume increase markedly – resulting in increased cardiac output and symptom improvement. Both women with first pregnancies and those with prior pregnancies usually handle pregnancies equally well. Pregnant women with POTS may require closer management than those with non-POTS pregnancies. Therefore, it's best to seek out a physician knowledgeable about POTS early in the pregnancy to help with management during the pregnancy. Your healthcare provider can be quite helpful with the POTS symptoms occurring during the pregnancy, associated with the delivery and those post-delivery.

Most pregnancies are delivered with regional anesthesia (epidural) without complications. During labor, "pushing" is the equivalent to the Valsalva maneuver. This "bearing down" causes an exaggerated early fall and later rise in pulse and blood pressure. If pulse and blood pressure do not return to baseline levels between contractions, some physicians consider that as an indication for a Cesarean delivery.

When Is Drug Therapy Utilized?

Unfortunately, not all POTS patients will respond to lifestyle adjustments. Many will require the addition of medications to their recovery program. Drug therapy is reserved for those who fail to respond adequately with behavioral changes.

There are no ideal drugs for POTS. In fact, drug therapy is often on a "trial basis" with the goal of alleviating symptoms. Single drugs are prescribed starting with a low dose and then the dose is gradually increased to avoid undesirable side effects. If the drug effect is beneficial, then the dose can be safely increased.

Those POTS patients with the severest symptoms will benefit from consultation with POTS specialists at major medical centers that specialize in managing POTS. The **POTS Resource Guide in Chapter 16** will help you locate major medical centers that conduct research on POTS and have published their results.

What Drug Therapy Is Available For Me?

Whereas each individual patient exhibits a unique combination of symptoms, no drug therapy is beneficial for all POTS patients. There are no FDA approved drugs for treatment of children, adolescents and adults with POTS. Therefore, all drugs prescribed for POTS are considered by the FDA to be "off label." "Off label" implies a drug has not been thoroughly investigated by the FDA. Thus, all of the drugs regularly prescribed for patients with POTS and found to be beneficial have not been approved for use in patients with POTS. The most frequently prescribed drugs utilized for POTS include:

Intravenous saline – intravenous saline is the best emergency therapy for POTS. Intravenous saline can rapidly expand blood volume, replace salt and reverse severe acute symptoms. A liter (1000 cc) of 0.9% saline contains 9 grams of salt. Intravenous saline may be required if one is acutely dehydrated or if oral intake is limited such as following surgery. Following surgery, many POTS patients require several liters of saline-rich intravenous fluids.

β-blockers – β-adrenergic blockers are utilized to slow down undesirable tachycardia when standing. Many POTS patients improve with β-blockers. However, β-blockers may not be well tolerated by others, as they may slow the heart rate so much as to worsen symptoms. Excessive slowing can impair brain blood flow, increase fatigue and exercise intolerance. Generally low doses work better than standard dosages.

Florinef (fludrocortisone) – a synthetic mineral-corticoid is utilized to encourage retention of salt and expansion of blood volume. However, it may cause fluid overload, hypokalemia (lowered potassium), headaches and/or high blood pressure.

Octreotide (somatostatin analog) – causes vasoconstriction of the splanchnic blood vessels (vessels feeding the abdominal organs). Octreotide is utilized to decrease pooling within the abdominal vessels in POTS patients with abdominal symptoms. In addition to reducing abdominal symptoms, it may improve orthostatic intolerance and tachycardia. Side effects can include worsening of headaches and blood sugar and thyroid hormone disturbances.

Midodrine – this peripheral alpha-1 adrenoreceptor agonist is the most frequently prescribed drug for POTS. It is utilized to increase venous constriction, decrease venous caliber and pooling in the lower limbs and reduce tachycardia. Whereas its action is short-lived, frequent dosing is required, usually taken multiple times per day. While some individuals can take it right before bedtime with no side effects, others cannot and may have trouble falling asleep. For those individuals, dosing within 4 hours of sleep is to be avoided. Frequent annoying side effects include scalp tingling, goose bumps and itching. More disturbing side effects include headaches, high blood pressure and difficulty with urination.

Keys to Your Recovery and POWER over POTS Are Learning How to:

- Avoid and overcome triggers

- Correct low blood volume

- Increase salt and fluid intake

- Reverse cardiovascular muscular deconditioning

- Reverse lower extremity muscular deconditioning

- Establish a strengthening and endurance exercise training program.

- Reduce stress

- Learn relaxing abdominal breathing

Keeping Recovery Records is an essential component of your recovery program. Consider utilizing the **Recovery Records** like those provided to **Monitor Your Progress**. Turn your stumbling blocks into **Stepping Stones to Recovery.**

Remember: Failing to Plan = Planning to Fail

Take Charge!!   Set Goals!!   You Too Can Recover!!

You Too Can Gain POWER over POTS!!

Chapter 10 describes **Illnesses That Can Co-Exist with POTS**

CHAPTER 10:

What Illnesses May Co-exist with POTS?

In many patients, additional medical conditions co-exist and further complicate the diagnosing and management of patients with POTS. Like POTS, chronic deconditioning is suspected of contributing to the severity of all of these illnesses. The following medical conditions are those that most frequently demonstrate abnormal HUTTs (head-up tilt tests) and can co-exist with POTS. In fact, some individuals have combinations of these conditions like chronic fatigue syndrome and POTS, Ehlers-Danlos syndrome (EDS) and POTS, and Mast Cell Activation Disorder (MCAD) and POTS. It's even possible for one individual to have three of these illnesses. MCAD, EDS and POTS regularly occur together in the same individuals. For some still unexplained reason, all of these conditions occur most frequently among females.

Although health care providers are aware of these debilitating illnesses individually, they rarely suspect their co-existence with POTS. For example, it becomes a major challenge for physicians trying to unravel the mysterious cause of episodic flushing of the neck, abdominal bloating, pain, fatigue and POTS symptoms experienced by a 13 year old healthy appearing young girl. Whereas these misunderstood illnesses frequently overlap, diagnosis and treatment becomes even more perplexing.

Many of these illnesses share the following disturbing and often difficult to explain symptoms:

- Headaches

- Dizziness

- Fatigue

- Abdominal discomfort

- Intellectual impairment

- Sleep disturbances

What usually happens, teens go to the doctor with such puzzling complaints and usually no physical abnormality can be discovered on examination.

Chronic Fatigue Syndrome (CFS) – An unexplained debilitating disorder characterized by new onset of profound fatigue lasting more than 6 months. CFS is more common in females than males and usually occurs at an older age than POTS adolescents. CFS occurs primarily among women between the ages of 30-50 with average onset around age 33. It's estimated that 1-2 million Americans suffer from CFS, and most remain undiagnosed.

CFS usually starts out with a flu-like illness with fever, headache, sore throat, swollen lymph nodes of the neck, muscle pains and severe fatigue. Even performance of a long list of medical tests is not helpful in establishing the CFS diagnosis, as all tend to be normal. Without the benefit of a reliable diagnostic test, making a diagnosis of CFS remains challenging. In fact, the diagnosis of CFS frequently becomes a diagnosis of exclusion – after excluding all other known medical possibilities.

While it is suspected of following an unspecified infectious illness, the cause of this medical condition remains unknown. Patients manifest headaches, concentration and memory impairment, muscle and joint pain. Many have sleep problems including trouble falling and staying asleep. Most crave sleep, tend to doze during the day and need to take frequent daytime naps. Many also demonstrate orthostatic intolerance similar to that among POTS patients.

Characteristically patients complain of lack of energy and fatigue that does not improve with rest or sleep. Following even mild exertion, pain, prolonged exhaustion and "crashing" are common. Similar "collapsing" can occur post emotional distress. Post-exertional fatigue and mental impairment can be particularly severe and incapacitating and can last for several days.

As lack of energy increases with the passage of time, so does deconditioning and muscle weakness. CFS affects patients' abilities to function in daily activities of school, work, household management and personal care. Impaired reasoning, depression, social, educational and occupational withdrawal follows. More recently CFS has received several new names: Systemic Exertion Intolerance Disease (**SEID**) and Myalgic Encephalomyelitis (**ME**) (describes the muscle pain and tenderness with inflammation of the brain and spinal cord). These new names describe the condition better than CFS which may trivialize the severity of the condition.

> *Ashley is a 38 year-old mother of 2 adolescents with a year-long history of chronic fatigue, headaches, dizziness, muscle and joint pains. Symptoms all began following a flu-like illness with several days of fever, headache and generalized body aching. Since, she has suffered with progressive and increasingly severe exhaustion. Her arms and legs constantly feel heavy and painful. The slightest activity causes worsening of her fatigue.*

Rest and sleep do not provide improvement. When standing, whether in the kitchen or just talking, she soon gets lightheaded and dizzy with blurred vision and must lie down immediately to prevent passing out. She has great difficulty caring for her family and preparing meals. She rarely leaves her home. Fortunately, her husband works from home and is able to take over the domestic responsibilities. Recently she was diagnosed with Myalgic Encephalomyelitis.

Ehlers-Danlos Syndrome (EDS) – A group of inherited disorders that affect the structure of collagens (the connective tissues) that support most body parts – primarily skin, eye, mucous membrane, nerve, cardiovascular, joint and bone structures. Estimated frequency is approximately 1/5000 births with 90% occurring among females. EDS appears to be a dominant hereditary trait, meaning if only one parent transmits the gene to you, you will manifest some of its characteristics. Connective tissues come in many specialized forms and serve to support, strengthen, bind and maintain the shapes of all organs. In EDS patients, the connective tissue structures are defective and weakened.

The most common manifestations of EDS are thin skin ("cigarette paper skin"), hyper-elastic skin (excessive skin stretching), drooping eyelids - easy bruising, bleeding and poor wound healing. Later in life the skin becomes soft and velvety. Thinning of the outer sclera layers of the eyes (whites of the eyes), mucous membranes of mouth and teeth can result in bluish-purple discoloration. Weakened walls of blood vessels can lead to frequent bruising. Patients with EDS also have defective healing of their connective tissues following surgery.

"Double-jointedness" is characteristic of EDS and can be observed in the fingers, wrists, shoulders, elbows, back, knees and toes. All joints can be affected, but those used most often like jaws, neck, shoulders, knees and feet are usually the first to present with pain. Joints that are extremely loose (double-jointed) are more prone to recurrent sprains. Because of weakened joint structure, EDS patients are more prone to repetitive stress injuries, dislocations, chronic arthritis and joint pains. Flat feet and fatigue are very frequent complaints.

Characteristic "double joints" include the abilities to: bend the little finger backward severely, bend the thumb backwards to touch the forearm, place palms of hands on floor without bending the knees, reach behind back and touch opposite ear, touch the nose with the tongue and over-extending the elbows and knees (bending backwards).

Some EDS patients take advantage of their loose ligaments and greater range of motion and excel as cheerleaders, gymnasts, dancers, swimmers, athletes and musicians. Many become famous winners, stars and champions in their respective fields. Unfortunately, due to overuse and abuse, they are prone to early debilitating arthritis.

Increasingly, a majority of EDS patients also exhibit gastrointestinal symptoms such as upper abdominal pain, gastro-intestinal reflux, early feeling of fullness, and disturbances of intestinal motility (nausea, bloating and vomiting). Lower abdominal symptoms include diarrhea and constipation. Defective collagen within the blood vessels and walls of the intestines alters their function – reducing muscular contractibility and slowing motility. Weakness of the tissues and muscles that strengthen the abdominal wall result in an increase in abdominal and inguinal (groin) hernias (tears in the supportive tissues of the abdominal wall). Defective collagen within the pelvic organs results in loss of pelvic support and abnormalities of bladder function, especially in women.

Every patient with EDS needs to be evaluated by a cardiologist to rule out the presence of abnormalities of heart valves and major vessels.

Frequently EDS and POTS occur together in the same patient. When combined, patients may experience greater weakening of valves and walls of veins leading to even greater venous pooling. Thus, they share POTS symptoms like headache, dizziness and "brain fog" Over-stretched and dilated veins encourage more exaggerated venous pooling. Further reduction in cardiac output leads to greater abdominal and more severe general POTS symptoms. Like POTS, EDS mostly affects females. A variety of genetic abnormalities have been discovered to be responsible for EDS. More recently, EDS is being referred to as the Joint Hypermobility Syndrome (**JHS**).

> *Mimi is a 20 year old college student on the lacrosse team. She had always taken pride in her ability to "touch her nose with her tongue," "reach behind her back and join both upper and lower hands" and "bend her thumb back flat against her forearm." However, she was not happy having to repeatedly miss several important lacrosse games due to painful severe sprained ankles. So, she consulted an orthopedist. She was shocked to discover that her "double-jointed condition" was also responsible for her repeated ankle injuries. The doctor showed Mimi she also demonstrated the characteristic "loose skin" of Ehlers-Danlos Syndrome. He explained that her loose ankle joint ligaments were contributing to her repeated ankle joint dislocations resulting in incapacitating pain and swelling. Fortunately, the doctor was able to prescribe braces that increased the stability of her ankles and permitted her to continue to participate in her beloved college lacrosse.*

Chiari malformation (CM) - A structural defect of the base of the skull resulting in a smaller bony opening than usual. This bony narrowing causes the base of the brain and brain stem to get tightly wedged in the opening connecting the brain to the spinal cord. The brain stem is the portion of the brain that joins the brain to the spinal cord. Many of the brain's automatic controls are located within the brain stem, for example heart rhythm, breathing, swallowing, sweating and coordination of speech, movement and balance.

Because the autonomic nervous system is localized within the region of the compressed brain stem, an assortment of dysautonomia symptoms are possible. The most frequent symptoms are headache, neck pain, dizziness, tingling, numbness, weakness in the arms, nausea, fatigue, trouble with swallowing, speaking, hand coordination, balance and walking. Symptoms may be brought on or made worse by straining, exercise, laughing and bending over. Symptoms suggestive of serious compression of the brain stem include tachycardia, sleep apnea, vomiting, swallowing problems and loss of bladder and bowel control.

CM occurs more frequently among females than males. Patients with EDS (hypermobility) have a greater incidence of CM. Apparently, children may be born with this condition, but symptoms do not appear until adolescence or adulthood (probably related to this growth stage). MRI imaging performed in the "upright position" can easily recognize this deformity and neurosurgery is the required corrective treatment.

Fibromyalgia (FM) – A chronic condition characterized by widespread musculoskeletal tenderness, pain, and stiffness accompanied by fatigue, sleep disturbances, memory and mood issues. Symptoms sometimes begin after a physical trauma, surgery, infection or significant psychological stress. Many FM patients also have POTS. The characteristic persistent disabling pain discourages movement, which promotes further weakness and pain when activity is attempted.

Anxiety-Panic Attacks-Hyperventilation – Unrecognized and untreated POTS can be quite stressful and is often associated with anxiety and panic attacks. Anxiety induces generalized muscular tightening – part of the preparation for battle response. Part of this general alarm system response is tightening of the diaphragm muscles, forcing breathing to now be primarily chest breathing. Stress can induce the sensation of shortness of breath which is actually rapid shallow chest breathing, also known as hyperventilation.

POTS patients generally have reduced quantities of body water (hypovolemia) and reduced body salt. Salt (sodium) plays an important role within the blood to maintain osmotic pressure and prevent loss of fluid into the surrounding tissues. To maintain homeostasis (internal balance), the kidneys are in charge of conserving as much water and salt as necessary.

Those experiencing hyperventilation frequently describe this shortness of breath feeling as "being unable to take a full breath." Diminished brain perfusion induced by standing encourages additional anxiety and the sensation of "needing to take deeper breathes" but, "being unable to take full breaths." Anxiety and chest breathing (hyperventilation) feed on each other. On the other hand, relaxed diaphragmatic breathing promotes calm. Inhalation is associated with negative thoracic (chest) pressure and the pulling in of blood from the major veins towards the heart. This attempt to improve cardiac output is a good thing. However, continued hyperventilation results in excessive blowing off of CO_2. This encourages reduced brain perfusion leading to worsening of symptoms.

The speeded-up metabolism induced by running encourages over-breathing in order to breathe in more oxygen and blow off increased carbon dioxide, which is a good thing. Unfortunately, over-breathing while not running, while inactive, results in blowing off more carbon dioxide than necessary with resultant reduced carbon dioxide dissolved in the blood. Hyperventilation results in blowing-off excess carbon dioxide and alters blood chemistry. This disturbance in the blood chemistry can further exaggerate POTS-like symptoms – including anxiety, nervousness, chest pain and tachycardia, heart palpitations, light-headedness, headaches, dizziness, coldness and tingling of the fingers and toes.

Treatment is learning how to substitute relaxing abdominal breathing for the anxiety and panic driven rapid shallow chest breathing of hyperventilation. Practicing relaxing abdominal breathing when not under stress is important so as to be able easily utilize relaxing breathing when stressed. (See **Tips for Learning Healthy Breathing** on Page 116)

> *Michael, a 21 year old college senior, with symptoms of frequent headaches, blurred vision and fatigue, was diagnosed with POTS the prior summer. While attending college, he periodically suffered with trouble concentrating and completing his assignments on time. Facing deadlines placed him under extreme stress. During the school year, he had to make three trips to the emergency room (ER) because of a smothering sensation, chest pain and shortness of breath. During the first two visits, he spent several hours in the ER, nothing abnormal was found and he was diagnosed with "panic attacks." Unable to sleep one night before a final exam, his chest pain and "fighting to get air" was so severe he was forced to make a fourth unplanned trip to the ER. This time an astute Emergency Room physician recognized that he was hyperventilating. The doctor taught Michael how to change his rapid shallow chest breathing into relaxing abdominal breathing. Afterwards, he practiced abdominal breathing every day and did not have any more emergency trips to the ER for the rest of the school year.*

Celiac Artery Compression Syndrome – a rare cause of abdominal symptoms caused by a fibrous band constricting the celiac artery and associated celiac nerve bundles that surround the celiac artery. The celiac artery arises from the aorta (main artery of the body delivering blood from the heart to the body) just below the diaphragm. The celiac artery and its branches bring nourishment to the stomach, pancreas and small intestines and the autonomic nerves regulate the function of the stomach, pancreas and small intestines. In patients with this syndrome, the fibrous band that connects the right and left diaphragms is too tight and squeezes both the artery and nerve bundles. Narrowing pinches the artery, reducing the blood supply to these organs, and pinches both sympathetic and parasympathetic nerve bundles, disrupting nervous signals to the upper abdominal organs. This syndrome is also called Median Arcuate Ligament Syndrome (MALS), named after the fibrous band that connects the right and left diaphragmatic muscles.

Symptomatic MALS occurs almost predominantly among young females. The reduced blood supply caused by the pinched artery results in patients complaining of mid and right sided upper abdominal pain. The disturbed nerve function results in chronic nausea, vomiting, diarrhea and loss of appetite. When this syndrome is present, this compression and associated symptoms are increased following eating a large meal, exercise, leaning forward or when standing and during exhalation. Because the pain following meals can be intense, patients often rapidly feel full, avoid eating and over time lose significant weight.

Sometimes the pinched artery creates a blowing noise (called a bruit) that can be heard in the upper abdomen with a stethoscope. The blowing noise may get louder during a deep breath when the diaphragm muscle moves down causing additional pinching of the celiac bundles or with expiration.

Many MALS patients with abdominal pain also have POTS and a third also have EDS. It is not unusual to observe the occurrence of MALS within both mother and daughter within the same family. Symptoms generally are present for years before being diagnosed. Once diagnosed, treatment usually consists of a simple surgical procedure that can be performed laparoscopically.

Mast Cell Activation Disorder (MCAD) – a newly recognized disease (or disorder) is caused by mast cell activation and is rarely considered or diagnosed. It frequently co-exists with POTS, again more frequently among females. Mast cells are members of the immune system. They are our first responders defending us against infections and toxins. Mast cells are found most plentiful in those tissues that are in contact with our environment, both internal and external.

Tissues with environmental contact include the skin, mucous membranes of lips, tongue, mouth, eyes, lungs and intestinal organs. But, mast cells are also present in lesser numbers in all other organs. When activated, mast cells release a wide assortment of defenders. Each plays a role in guarding us, but each can also contribute to disturbing allergic and inflammatory symptoms. The disturbing symptoms experienced by patients with MCAD include episodic attacks affecting most organ systems:

- General – allergies, fatigue, fever, weakness, headache, environmental sensitivities, insomnia
- Skin – flushing (head and neck), hives, itching, swelling (angioedema) of eyes, lips, throat, hands, genitals and other areas and skin writing (dermatographia)
- Mucous membranes – nasal stuffiness, congestion, sinusitis
- Eyes – sore, red, itchy, difficulty focusing
- Lungs – wheezing, shortness of breath, asthma, coughs
- Intestinal organs – colicky abdominal pain, cramping, nausea, vomiting, bloating, diarrhea, enlarged spleen, abnormal liver function tests
- Cardiovascular – tachycardia, palpitations, fainting, low or elevated blood pressure
- Musculoskeletal – muscle, bone, chest and joint pain,
- Neuropsychiatric – headache, anxiety, dizziness, lightheadedness, "brain fog"

Dermatographia (skin writing) is an interesting phenomenon. A line of welts and hives can be created by pressing or rubbing the skin with a blunt object. The occurrence of skin writing is common in MCAD, but also occurs in a variety of allergic conditions. For show, MCAD patients can have someone scratch a numbered answer on their back, cover with a shirt and then ask another person a mathematical problem for which the answer has already been written. Then, lifting their shirt they can magically reveal the numbered answer written as raised hives.

More and more patients with MCAD are reporting abdominal symptoms - cramping, pain, nausea and diarrhea. While abdominal symptoms are common even among children, their frequency increases into adulthood.

Triggers play an important role in initiating mast cell attacks. Triggers can be emotional, physical and chemical. Physical triggers include heat, cold, sunlight, rubbing and exercise. Chemical triggers include food, drinks, fragrances, aspirin, alcohol, toxins and drugs. Even menstruation can trigger an attack. Following attacks, patients feel exhausted and may need to sleep for hours. Severe reactions like those to bee venom can be life threatening.

To support a diagnosis of MCAD, try to relate the onset of a specific attack to a recent activity that may have triggered mast cell activation. When one can directly associate a recent trigger to an attack, avoidance of attacks becomes possible. For example, if taking hot showers causes generalized itching and hives, taking showers with cooler water makes sense. If symptoms follow eating cheese or yeast-risen breads or taking aspirins for a headache, restricting those becomes important.

MCAD frequently co-exists with both POTS and Ehlers-Danlos syndrome. Mild symptoms generally start early in childhood, and symptoms progressively increase in frequency and worsen with age. Diagnosis can be made by measuring elevated tryptase levels in the blood (within 4 hours) and methylhistamine and other products of mast cell metabolism in the urine (within 4 hours immediately after an attack). Therefore, to confirm an attack, it is necessary to demonstrate normal levels between attacks and elevated levels of these markers immediately after an occurrence. Ingestion of wine, seafood and soy sauce can cause false positive results for histamine.

Similar to POTS, patients with MCAD also experience headaches, dizziness, "brain fog" and tachycardia. Unlike POTS, patients with MCAD can develop both elevated and lowered blood pressure during attacks.

Antihistamines are frequently the first drugs prescribed and may minimize the milder symptoms of mast cell activation. However, treatment can often require use of a variety of symptom-specific medications prescribed by a mast cell disease specialist, if you can find one.

> Growing up, Ellen had a history of being allergic to a number of antibiotics producing generalized hives. Beginning at age 12, she noted sudden warmth and redness of her face and neck shortly after eating. Later that year, she began developing severe attacks of cramps and diarrhea associated with stress. At age 14, being around cats and dogs caused hives and wheezing, and her bouts of cramps and diarrhea occurred more frequently. At the same time, she grew several inches, and started complaining of tachycardia, dizziness, headaches and trouble concentrating when upright. At age 16, she noted recurrent bouts of red, itchy swelling of her lips and eyelids associated with heart racing – all without any explanation.
>
> When she finally reported her story to a physician, he confirmed the presence of dermatographia (skin writing) and suggested that she might have mast cell activation disorder. Blood and urine testing following an episode of hives and wheezing confirmed the diagnosis. In addition, a

HUTT was positive for POTS. She was instructed to keep a diary of her meals and activities looking for triggers. Later she experimented with a few antihistamines, to find the one that best controlled her symptoms. For POTs, she started leg strengthening exercises and increased her fluids and salt intake.

Multiple Sclerosis (MS) – an autoimmune disease wherein the body's immune system attacks the nervous system. Typical symptoms are fatigue, visual disturbances, numbness, tingling, pain, weakness, impaired balance and muscle coordination. Slurred speech, loss of balance and difficulty walking are characteristic signs of MS, but not of POTS. Symptoms can be either transient or permanent. MS occurs primarily among women between the ages 20 to 50.

Patients with MS may also have involvement of the autonomic nervous system. Some lose the ability to constrict the veins in the legs. When this occurs, which is frequent, patients suffering with MS develop POTS symptoms. Similar to POTS, they develop upright-related dizziness, palpitations, visual disturbances and near fainting. Treating their POTS can be beneficial for those with both MS and POTS.

Post-Concussion Syndrome – disturbed brain function following a head injury. Not only did pre-existing POTS symptoms worsen following a head injury, but frequently individuals with post-concussion syndrome develop POTS symptoms and demonstrate a positive Tilt Table Test.

Chapter 11 describes some **Illnesses That Are Often Confused with POTS.**

What Illnesses Are Often Confused with POTS?

Many other medical conditions share symptoms and/or signs with POTS and are often confused with POTS. This group of illnesses needs to be considered among the differential diagnosis and ruled out before making a definitive diagnosis of POTS. Among the most frequent medical conditions confused with POTS, the following illnesses need to be excluded by your healthcare provider:

Adolescent fatigue – Adolescents have too much to do, too many places to see and too many friends to spend time with. With so many demands on their time, sleep often goes to the bottom of the priority list. As many as 20% of adolescents are sleep deprived and complain of daily fatigue that is not alleviated by rest or sleep.

Anemia – Low red blood cell concentrations can result in diminished oxygenation of bodily tissues with resultant shortness of breath, rapid heart rate and fatigue. Anemia can be acute due to blood loss or chronic due to a variety of blood or metabolic disorders. The presence of anemia can be easily checked by a simple blood test.

Dysautonomia - Describes a group of disorders involving failure of the autonomic nervous system that controls the involuntary actions of the body. It can consist of either or both the sympathetic and parasympathetic components of the nervous system. Dysautonomias affect many millions of people and occur more commonly among females. Neurocardiogenic syncope (fainting) and POTS are the most common disorders of the autonomic nervous system. Other primary dysautonomias include multiple system atrophy, autonomic dysreflexia, baroreflex failure and familial dysautonomia. Secondary dysautonomias occur with chronic conditions such as diabetes, rheumatoid arthritis, multiple sclerosis, alcoholism and Parkinson's disease. Most share typical POTS symptoms including heart rhythm and blood pressure abnormalities, lightheadedness and fainting.

Eating disorders – Eating disorders occur most commonly among young females, but also occur among young males. Individuals with eating disorders experience reduced fluid and food intake and/or purging. All are associated with volume depletion (hypovolemia) and POTS-like symptoms including chronic fatigue, lightheadedness and dizziness. In addition, unlike POTS, they often demonstrate postural hypotension (low blood pressure) and depression.

Encephalitis – An acute serious infection of the brain characterized by new onset headache, fever, tachycardia, drowsiness and fatigue. Most bouts of encephalitis are caused by viral infections.

Fatigue – Lack of energy and feeling tired are common complaints in the general population. Sleep deprivation, especially common among college students, is usually blamed for feeling tired during the day. Fatigue may accompany depression, minor as well as major illnesses such as diabetes, arthritis, heart, lung and kidney disorders.

Gastrointestinal infections - Postural intolerance and tachycardia are frequently associated with a bout of gastroenteritis (severe nausea and vomiting and/or diarrhea) due to excessive fluid loss. Here, the severe fluid loss reduces circulating blood volume and can mimic POTS symptoms. The vomiting and diarrhea, with the loss of fluids and salts, and reduced blood volume that occurs post gastro-intestinal viral infections often leads to similar postural tachycardia, fatigue, headaches, lightheadedness, and abdominal disturbances. However, in cases following gastro-intestinal infections, bodily fluids become depleted, blood pressure falls significantly and causing individuals to experience fainting when attempting to resume an upright posture. Unlike POTS, in otherwise healthy individuals, improvement by replacement of lost fluids and salts leads to a complete recovery within days. Low blood pressure and fainting, as seen with severe intestinal infections, are not considered to be characteristic symptoms of POTS.

Gastroparesis – A chronic disorder of the stomach characterized by sluggish stomach emptying. Rather than an obstructing lesion, the cause is dysfunction of the nervous control of stomach motility (dysautonomia). Gastroparesis (sluggish stomach emptying) results in unpredictable absorption and passage of food. Symptoms include post-meal fullness, nausea, upper abdominal pain and vomiting. Gastroparesis primarily occurs in young females and diabetics. When prolonged, weight loss, weakness and chronic fatigue eventually follows.

Hypertension – Elevated blood pressure is a common medical condition. Hypertension occurs most commonly among older adults, not adolescents. Untreated, patients with hypertension commonly also experience headaches and rapid heart rate.

Infections – Most infections are associated with fever, tachycardia and fatigue. Some examples include Lyme disease, infectious mononucleosis and influenza. Each specific infection attacks a unique group of bodily organs and specific tests are available to help make the diagnosis.

Irritable Bowel Syndrome (IBS) – IBS is a very common condition primarily occurring among children and young women causing considerable abdominal complaints and disability. These patients suffer with severe unexplained abdominal pain, nausea and mainly diarrhea- or constipation-related symptoms. In spite of extensive testing, no abnormalities have been discovered to explain the cause. Some investigators suspect this is another example of dysfunction of the gastrointestinal autonomic nervous system - automatic control of digestive organs. More recently, some patients labeled as having IBS have been later diagnosed with Ehlers-Danlos Syndrome (EDS) EDS or Hypermobility Joint Syndrome (HJS) as it is now called. When checked for the characteristic loose skin and double-jointed signs, patients with IBS often turn out to have EDS instead. Many also have positive Head-Up Tilt Tests and co-existing symptoms of POTS.

Lyme disease – An acute tick-bite induced infection characterized initially by chills, fever, headache, fatigue, muscle pain, a single joint arthritis and a distinctive "bullseye rash" at the site of the causative tick bite. Lyme disease can be an acute short term illness or become a chronic prolonged illness that can attack the brain or heart. Diagnosis remains difficult because more patients demonstrate a generalized rash than the distinctive "bullseye rash." In addition, the specific blood test is not as reliable as desired. Antibiotic treatment of the early phase of the infection is much more effective than treatment of the late chronic phase of Lyme disease. Too often unexplained illnesses are labeled as "chronic Lyme disease" and are treated inappropriately with prolonged intravenous antibiotics.

Marfan's syndrome (MFS) – Disease caused by a defective gene that makes abnormal connective tissue throughout the body. Common features easily recognizable of the defective connective tissue are a tall thin body, long arms, legs and fingers, chest caved-in or sticks-out, crowded teeth and flexible joints. Eye abnormalities include severe nearsightedness, dislocated lenses, glaucoma and cataracts. These characteristic physical signs are easily recognizable by medical practitioners. The most serious connective tissue abnormalities are related to weakened walls of the aorta (main blood vessel that carries blood from the heart to the entire body) that can easily separate and tear.

Meningitis - An acute serious infection of the brain characterized by new onset headache, fever, tachycardia, drowsiness and fatigue. In contrast, meningitis infections are caused by bacteria, for which more effective therapy is available than for viral encephalitis.

Migraine headaches – Migraines are repetitive episodic attacks of severe headaches associated with nausea and frequently vomiting. Usually the headaches are preceded by an aura (bright lights or unpleasant smells), are one-sided and are associated with an increased sensitivity to light, sound or smell. Onset of headaches is often related to triggers such as specific foods, beverages, activities, bright lights, odors, changes in sleep patterns, changes in weather, etc. For each person, a specific headache pattern develops and tends to be repetitive with subsequent attacks. Migraine headaches are most common among females, especially during menses and can be quite disabling.

Multiple system atrophy (MSA) – A rare rapidly progressive degenerative neurologic disease characterized by failure of many components of the autonomic nervous system occurring primarily in older adults.

Orthostatic hypotension – Orthostatic hypotension (low blood pressure associated with standing) is defined as systolic blood pressure that declines 30 mm or more within 3 minutes of standing upright. Short-lived orthostatic hypotension with transient lightheadedness can occur during standing. Orthostatic hypotension is a more common problem among the elderly resulting in brain hypoperfusion, fainting, falls and injuries. More severe forms with brain hypoperfusion are often associated with many other medical conditions, but not usually with POTS. Most commonly it occurs with loss of fluids or blood, infectious diseases, medications and a variety of chronic diseases like diabetes, heart or kidney failure.

Panic attacks – When stressed, we respond to danger by unconsciously taking rapid shallow chest breaths, also known as hyperventilation. Over-breathing during running or fighting is necessary in order to inhale extra oxygen and exhale the excessive carbon dioxide produced during strenuous muscular activity. Unfortunately, over-breathing while not running, results in blowing off excessive carbon dioxide. With reduced carbon dioxide dissolved in the blood, the disturbed acid-base blood chemistry causes anxiety, nervousness, chest pain, tachycardia, heart palpitations, lightheadedness, headaches, dizziness, tingling or cold fingers and toes. Most frequently, attacks are associated with difficulty breathing, feelings of terror and impending doom. Anxiety-induced panic attacks are frequent triggers for trips to the Emergency Room. The best treatment is learning relaxing abdominal breathing.

Pheochromocytoma – A rare endocrine tumor that produces excessive adrenaline-like hormones and presents with heart palpitations, headaches, excessive sweating and high blood pressure. Most frequently, these symptoms are episodic, but they can also be constant. These tumors can occur in many sites within the body and can be either benign or malignant. Locating the site of the original tumor can be a diagnostic challenge.

Post-concussion syndrome - Head injuries, even those considered insignificant, can injure the brain. The associated symptoms can be identical to those of POTS – headache, dizziness, blurred vision, confusion, memory loss, nausea and vomiting. Slurred speech and loss of balance are not usually POTS-related, therefore require immediate medical evaluation. Blows to the head can result in damage that may result in acute symptoms or symptoms that persist for prolonged periods of time. Reporting the history of a head injury to your healthcare provider is always important, as symptoms may only become apparent after a prolonged time delay.

Pregnancy-associated dizziness, lightheadedness and fainting – Many pregnant women late in pregnancy experience these symptoms when lying flat on their back. Most often, these symptoms are caused by pressure of the enlarged uterus obstructing the main vein that returns blood back to the heart. All of these symptoms can be prevented or relieved by simply sleeping on one's side during the third trimester of pregnancy. This maneuver removes the pressure of the enlarged uterus on the main abdominal vein. These symptoms may resemble those of POTS, as the pressure on the main vein diminishes venous return back to the heart and reduces cardiac output. Similar symptoms can occur when pregnancy is complicated by severe anemia (reduced number of circulating red blood cells).

Psychiatric disorders – Anorexia, bipolar disorder, depression and schizophrenia can present with chronic fatigue, headaches and impaired cognitive functioning. The symptoms associated with these conditions should be easily distinguished from POTS.

Substance abuse – Many illicit drugs can cause "brain fog," tachycardia, headaches, sweating etc. that resemble the symptoms associated with POTS. Most drugs of abuse have profound and harmful effects upon the sympathetic nervous and cardiovascular systems.

Thyroid disease – An overactive thyroid gland can cause tachycardia, palpitations and weight loss, while an underactive thyroid gland can cause slow heart rate, mental and physical fatigue. Taking excessive thyroid hormone pills can mimic the same symptoms as an overactive thyroid gland. The symptoms associated with these conditions should be easily distinguished from POTS.

Vasovagal syncope – Usually emotional-stress-induced fainting is associated with pain, stress, seeing blood, being in a hospital or a sudden emotional shock. This type of fainting is caused by parasympathetic over activity with resultant rapid fall in both heart rate and blood pressure.

Corrective therapy usually consists of laying the patient down flat with elevation of the legs. Usually this kind of fainting bout clears as fast as it came on. Only rarely, does it persist for a period of time. When it is repetitive, a more thorough medical evaluation is necessary.

Chapter 12 explains **Strategies for Special Situations for Adolescents with POTS**

CHAPTER 12:

Strategies for Special Situations - Adolescents with POTS

Poor School Performance

> *POTS turned Karen's college life upside-down. Plagued by headaches, dizziness and trouble concentrating, she became depressed. For this 19 year old, everyday college tasks like keeping track of home-work assignments, appointments and studying for tests became a nightmare. She was unable to stand and wash her hair or go on shopping trips. Her school performance gradually deteriorated. This previously high achiever was now failing classes. Even her fellow students were unable to understand her worsening confusion.*

How Does One Seek out a Supportive Team?

While understandably difficult, going to and staying in school is best for students with POTS. Getting back into a normal, regular routine can make students feel better by distracting them from their symptoms and keeping them in the social scene with their peers. However, just because it's better to be in school, doesn't mean that it's easy. Walking in hallways, sitting in class, and focusing on schoolwork are all challenges for the student with POTS. But, having a supportive group of parents, educators and friends can help.

Parents can help find an advocate in the school administration to work with the student to develop a modified learning plan. It may be the Learning Support Specialist, school nurse or the guidance counselor. The best option would be a team approach that includes all three. Request a meeting with the student's advocates in the school to help form a plan. It is essential to obtain the administration's support. Administrators can help by talking to teachers to explain the class accommodations that may be needed. Plan to meet with the teachers on a one to one basis to explain to them what POTS is and how it affects learning. It will be important for you to advocate for yourself. Some teachers will probably be more supportive than others. Your student's teachers need to understand that your child is not lazy or deliberately trying to get out of class or doing their assignments.

Teachers may not be receptive to the student's needs if they are interrupting their class to explain why they need to get up and walk around. These conversations should take place outside of class time with a respectful tone to the teacher. Sometimes, teachers aren't always receptive to kids with POTS and think they are making excuses so that they can be disruptive or get out of class. If one is having a hard time getting a teacher to understand your student's needs, you may need to enlist the help of your guidance counselor, learning support specialist or school nurse to back you up. Often, parents may have to get involved as well.

Getting up at the same time every morning helps establish a regular sleeping schedule and routine. Students should strive to eat healthy meals at regular times during the day. The more consistent one's sleeping, eating and exercising schedule, the more control one will have over their life and the better they will feel. However, if a student has been out of school for a while, it may be helpful to return gradually. Accommodations can mean coming in for only an hour or two each day and gradually increasing up to a longer day. Sometimes it's hard to get up and moving early in the morning, so some students take an elective or a study hall as the first class in the morning. Thus, if the student arrives late, he/she won't miss an essential class.

Are School Accommodations Available to Help?

Here is a list of accommodations that students with POTS have found helpful. Have your parents work with your school advocates to establish permission for these in your classes. Make sure the teachers are aware of these measures before returning to the classroom.

- Try to arrange for a designated note taker for each class period. This is helpful for when a student misses a class due to illness or doctor's appointments. Also, brain fog and memory loss affects many adolescents with POTS. Having a set of notes is essential in coping with these symptoms and can help keep a student caught up in the classroom.

- Request that teachers allow access to drinks and salty snacks whenever needed. Request liberal leave to use the bathroom. This does not mean one can go wander the halls when bored to go see friends. One can't take advantage of these privileges or teachers will complain about one's behavior and start taking privileges away.

- Teachers need to be aware that sitting for prolonged periods of time is counter-productive to POTS as it decreases circulation. Explain the need to be allowed to stand in the back of the room and march in place for a few minutes or exit the room and take a quick brisk walk or do some of the leg exercises described in this book to get one's blood flowing. Again, don't go for an extended walk around the school and start chatting with people. Don't get caught and have to start explaining to the staff that the student isn't actually goofing off.

- The school nurse can be a great resource. If other kids in school have had POTS, the nurse will be familiar with the medical needs of POTS students. If your student is the first student with POTS, take some time to educate the nurse about what the family is going thorough. Sometimes it will be up to the parents to educate the nurse. And after all the experience gained from medical tests and appointments, parents probably understand POTS better than anyone. Many students with POTS have had their symptoms misunderstood and challenged, so it is always helpful to have a knowledgeable school nurse who can offer support. The nurse may be able to have an area in her room where she can store beverages and salty snacks for your student. She may also have a quiet area where one can come and lie down for a short period of time if necessary. But, while tempting, students should not spend the day sleeping in the nurse's office. The goal should always be to return to the classroom.

- Sometimes, students have a designated "buddy" from each class who can escort the student to the nurse's office if they are feeling unsteady or dizzy. This way they won't fall or faint on the way to getting help.

- For some patients with POTS, the symptoms make learning incredibly difficult. One of the most difficult symptoms that can impact one's schoolwork is "brain fog" and memory loss. If this is one of your student's major POTS symptoms, one might try taking some classes such as art, music, photography and film. For example, sometimes a school will offer an English class that is film based. Math and science are particularly difficult because the classes build on material learned the day before. Reading can cause headaches and getting one's thoughts together for writing can be daunting. One eleventh grader said that the task of writing felt like "trying to ride a unicycle across the ocean." Just remember, as a student begins treatment, stick to one's food, sleep and exercise plan, one will begin to feel better and symptoms will lessen. For one student with severe memory loss, after he began following his treatment plan, his memory improved significantly after about six months and was almost completely better after just over a year. Unfortunately with POTS, treatment doesn't work the same as with penicillin and a strep throat where you take a pill and you're better in ten days. POTS symptoms will take longer to get better, but will improve if one sticks with her/his treatment plan.

While Adam, age 17, did require some special accommodations from his high-school teachers, he did go on and graduate. Luckily, he improved enough to be a full time college student and also serve as his college's mascot for basketball, hockey, volleyball and lacrosse. Being a mascot required running, dancing and jumping inside a 20 degree warmer costume for 3+ hours. He gained enough stamina to wear this 35 pound costume, entertain his classmates and pump-up their college spirit for 4 years. Not only can one overcome POTS, but former debilitated POTS patients can accomplish extremely physically demanding upright challenges. Proof is seeing Adam as his home team's mascot "working the crowd." Adam proved that one can gain POWER over POTS!

Are Accommodations Available to Help with Standardized Testing Issues?

Standardized testing is challenging as well. Talk to the college counselor well before the test so that the student can apply for accommodations when taking the SAT, ACT, AP and other tests. Some of the available accommodations are allowing for extra test time, extra breaks and the ability to take the test over several sittings instead of all at one time.

How Do Students Cope with Social Challenges when Returning to School after A Medical Absence?

For many reasons, going back to school can be very hard. Aside from trying to catch up with the workload, fitting back in socially can also be a challenge. Let's face it. Some kids aren't nice. They weren't nice before your student had POTS and they might not be nice now. Many of them may not change, but maybe a few will change and surprise you. One's focus should be on staying positive and using one's energy to get well, not fixating on the haters.

It is also common for some kids to call students out as fakers or attention seekers. When trying to get back to school while feeling awful, it can be very upsetting to have kids at school tease or call one a "faker" or "drama queen". Listed below are some ideas one can do to minimize the teasing, but ultimately it will be up to your student to ignore some of it.

How Do Students Re-Connect With Friends?

Most kids have a small group of close friends, even if it's just one or two friends, whom the student knows has their back. Focus on them. Share one's medical information with them so they understand what's happening. And let them know that your student may need a little extra support when they are having a rough day. If due to feeling badly, your student hasn't been around their friends for a while, let them know that your student is coming back to school and is looking forward to seeing them. If your student hasn't been in school for a while, some friends may have moved on and are hanging out with new kids. Try and join in with the new kids, it might be an opportunity for your student to meet some new kids too.

Sometimes people want to share all their medical information and what they've been going through. The POTS explanation may be long and involved and be more information than people can understand. Sometimes, people aren't ready to hear it all - not because they don't care, but they might not have time to listen or they have their own struggles and worries. When someone asks "What's wrong with you?" or "Why haven't you been in school?" Go for the short answer. It is perfectly reasonable to say something like, "I've been diagnosed with a condition called POTS. It affects my autonomic nervous system. There are automatic body functions that I can't control like heart rate, circulation and oxygen to my brain. But I'm getting treatment and I'm doing better!" Then change the topic and say things like "What's new with you?" or "What's going on in your life?" or talk about a new movie or TV show. The more typical a conversation one can have with friends and the less time one has to focus on how bad POTS makes one feel, the faster relationships in school will get back to normal. People do care, they just don't want to hear about other people's symptoms all of the time.

How to Best Plan Responses to Friends?

Going back the first day to school can be nerve wracking. Some kids like to rehearse with their family what they are going to say to people when they go back to school. Students should expect to be bombarded with all kinds of questions, so it's a good idea to have a plan. Have planned responses, so as not to have to quickly think about what to say and lessen the anxiety associated with going back to school.

No matter how well one plans or how many friends one has, there will always be someone who just doesn't get it or says things that are just annoying and stupid. Unfortunately, this is life and one needs to learn how to deal with or ignore these comments and behaviors. Saying something nasty back is useless, and it won't change others. The best thing one can do is just say something short like "Whatever" and move on. Students should focus on spending time with true friends, people who get it, and those who are supportive.

Are There Helpful Travel Tips?

Long rides or flights can be problematic as they discourage blood circulating up from the legs. Get up and walk around. Try and do leg exercises. It is good to have exercises that you can do while sitting and standing. Wherever possible, fly direct without stop-overs thus shortening the travel day.

It is important to be well hydrated before plane trips because air travel promotes dehydration. Drink lots of water before planned plane trips, starting a few days before so as to start the trip well hydrated. Also bring water or a beverage along when traveling. Sometimes if plane rides are bumpy, the flight attendants stop beverage service and they might not get to you. Therefore, make sure to bring plenty of drinks of your own.

How to Plan Ahead for Special Occasions

Just because one feels terrible, doesn't mean one has to miss special occasions. Planning ahead for such events and trips can really prevent setbacks in one's recovery. Many doctors who treat teens with POTS report that 4 or 5 days after New Year's Eve, Prom weekends, the Fourth of July and Halloween, they get an increase in phone calls from parents saying that their children, who were doing well, have now taken a turn for the worse. Going off a scheduled routine even for one night can lead to a rough following week. It doesn't mean that one can't participate in these special late night events; but it does require the need to plan ahead for them. If one knows that they will be up late for a special occasion, one needs to get extra rest in the days leading up to the event. Stick to a strict exercise plan and don't miss a day even if one doesn't feel like it. If one can grab a nap the day of the big event, that can help too. But, the best thing one can do for oneself is to stick to one's rest, fluids and exercise plan. How one feels after the special event is related to how well they prepare for it during the week before.

Regaining the Power of Fun, Joy, Laughter and Happiness

What Does Your Mind-Body Know?

POTS patients regularly deal with excessive obstacles and challenges. This inner turmoil and emotional distress can leave its mark on one's health. Evidence continues to accumulate that the brain talks to the body and the body talks to the brain. Inner messages influence both how one feels and one's body physiology. Negative emotions result in the outpouring of powerful body chemicals that can make you feel worse. Likewise, healthy emotions can help encourage healing. Happiness may be hard to measure, but your mind-body machine knows when you're enjoying yourself and runs better on pleasure. How often one feels good and laughs has a major impact on one's overall wellbeing. Throughout history, joy, laughter and hope have impressed scientists and scholars as being good for one's health.

Happiness comes from perceiving and delighting in the many enriching opportunities life offers for joy and laughter. Thinking about present pleasurable experiences, recalling prior happy times and planning future fun, help "accentuate your positive" and 'eliminate your negative" inner thoughts. Even small satisfying moments in a day can uplift one's mood, facilitate relaxation and turn on healthy physiologic changes. Fun, joy and laughter can create lasting pleasant memories for you and those who share happy times with you.

Where Do We Find Fun, Joy, Laughter and Happiness?

Think positive. No emotion has greater impact on outcome and happiness. Start off and end each day with positive thoughts. One of the most popular songs of 1945 was Harold Arlen and Johnny Mercer's "Accentuate the Positive" that promoted emphasizing positive thoughts and actions and getting rid of negative thoughts and actions.

Songs and music offer artistic, entertainment and emotional values that are quite complex. Listening to music can be stimulating and exciting or relaxing and sedating. Each listener's unique preferences and mood influence both the selections and reactions to songs and music. Brain processing of music is extensive, the creative function is focused in the right hemisphere and the relaxing function is focused in the left hemisphere. Music can play a positive therapeutic role in anxiety, stress, pain and sleep management and alleviating nausea and vomiting associated with chemotherapy. Addition of imagery to music results in even greater effectiveness. Songs and music have magical powers – not only to modify mood, but also to modulate physiology.

T-shirts, buttons, balloons, coffee mugs, hats, cartoons and similar items decorated with amusing words, pictures and funny messages can make you laugh and lift your spirits. Each day, try to expose yourself to a multitude of funny messages. Take advantage of the joy and laughter each can deliver.

Funny memes and inspirational quotes are abundantly available online. They offer a wonderful way to lighten your mood and help you laugh even when you feel miserable. Select several of your favorites and place them where you can conveniently see them often to help change your mood into a better one when you are struggling.

Activities like cuddling with pet animals, watching or participating in preferred sports, enjoying favorite movies, television programs or theater productions and humorous readings can provide pleasure. There are many new board and card games available that are fun and guarantee you will laugh when you play them. Even favorable family gatherings, traveling, giving to charity, and hugs, all can go a long way to add fun and happiness to your life.

> Think positive. No emotion has greater impact on outcome and happiness. Start off and end each day with positive thoughts.

Can Friends Help Me Recover?

Don't forget the power of good friends. All of us benefit from social support that helps us cope with adversity. All of us thrive on friendships that pick us up when we're down. Even William Shakespeare recognized the value of friendship.

"A friend is one that knows you as you are,

Understands where you've been,

Accepts what you've become,

And still gently allows you to grow."

It's extremely helpful to surround yourself throughout the day with opportunities to employ these mental health tools. Each can provide you with
ways to move your distressful thoughts to delightful feelings. All of them
can lighten up your inner messages resulting in a calmer brain and health-
ier body. Start collecting tools like these to add to your fun, joy, laughter
and happiness. Collect funny T-shirts, watch hilarious movies with friends,
listen to your favorite comediennes, read books of humorous jokes and
memorize a few humor mantras. Daily doses will have positive impacts
on your health and shift your physiology from negative to positive. All can
contribute to POWER over POTS!

Chapter 13 explains **Strategies for Special Situations-Supportive
Parenting of Adolescents with POTS**

Strategies for Special Situations- Supportive Parenting of Adolescents with POTS

Steps To Encourage School Success – Overcoming Roadblocks

Easing the Return to School

If adolescents have been out of school for a while, returning to school gradually can be helpful. Ideally, make arrangements for your student to come in for only an hour or two each day and gradually increase their time in school. Some modifications can be made to your child's school day as well. However, you will need to explain to your child that while all of these modifications are necessary for them, they need to be careful to not abuse the privileges or be disruptive to classes in anyway.

Getting up at the same time every morning helps establish a regular sleeping schedule and routine. Strive for students to eat healthy meals at regular times during the day. The more consistent one's sleeping and eating schedule, the more control one has over their life and the better the student will feel.

Don't forget the power of good friends.
All of us benefit from social support
that helps us cope with adversity.
All of us thrive on friendships that
pick us up when we're down.

Phasing in the Return to Classes

If possible, encourage her/him to take an elective or a study hall as the first class in the morning. Sometimes it's hard to get up and moving early in the morning. This way, if the student arrives late, they won't miss an essential class. Sometimes it is possible to arrange your child's schedule to start the school day later on a regular basis by grouping all the important classes together, eliminating electives and winding up with a shorter class day. As the student feels stronger, electives can always be added back into the schedule.

Try to arrange for a designated note taker for each class period. That way, your child has the notes from each class in case they have to miss a class due to illness or doctor's appointments. Also, brain fog and memory loss affects many adolescents with POTS. Having a set of notes is extremely helpful in coping with symptoms and helps in keeping up with the class-room work.

Request that teachers allow your child free access to drinks and salty snacks whenever needed. Also, request liberal leave to use the bathroom. Teachers need to be aware that sitting for prolonged periods of time is counter-productive to POTS, as it decreases circulation. Students need to be allowed to stand in the back of the room and march in place for a few minutes or exit the room, take a quick brisk walk or do some of the leg exercises described in this book to get their blood flowing.

Enlisting the Help of the School Nurse

An educated school nurse can be an invaluable resource. Many times, POTS symptoms occur initially while the student is at school. Often the school nurse is the first person your child will have contact with when the student begins to experience symptoms. Thus, school nurses can be the first ones to identify POTS symptoms in students. But, they will only be able to do so if they've had experience with other POTS students. If the school nurse has had previous students with POTS, they will usually recognize the symptoms and offer support to the student. If they haven't had any previous students with POTS, it will be up to your child to educate the nurse.

Many students with POTS have had their symptoms misunderstood and challenged, so it is always helpful to have a knowledgeable school nurse who can offer compassion and be an advocate for your child. The school nurse can also be integral in helping the administrators, guidance staff and faculty work together to come up with an accommodating educational plan for your child. The nurse may be able to have an area in her room where she can store beverages and salty snacks. She may also have a quiet area where your student can come and lie down for a short period of time, if necessary. While tempting, your child should not spend the day sleeping in the nurse's office. The goal should always be to return to class.

Have your school nurse look at the physical layout of the school. Check if any accommodations can be made to minimize the physical stress on your student. Useful accommodations can include grouping your child's classes near each other, providing an elevator pass and allowing extra time in between classes when long distanced apart. Some students with POTS have needed to get around during the day using a wheelchair.

Sometimes, students have a designated "buddy" from each class who can escort your student to the nurse's office if they are feeling unsteady or dizzy. A buddy can help prevent falling or fainting on the way to getting help.

Dealing With "Brain Fog"

While some cardiologists suspected Brandon may have POTS, none of the specialists consulted were able to attribute his severe amnesia to his POTS or dysautonomia. At the time, none of the physicians caring for Brandon realized that the brain hypoperfusion of POTS could cause such significant amnesia (short-term memory loss).

When evaluated at a major medical center, they confirmed that Brandon, aged 16, had a diagnosis of POTS. Even more important was learning that 10 % or more of the POTS patients referred to that major medical center also suffer with amnesia (short-term memory loss). At that medical center he received extensive training in the self-management of POTS – how to take back his life. The doctors assured Brandon that the proscribed rehabilitation program could, with time and dedication, improve the amnesia and his other symptoms.

Once Brandon's diagnosis was confirmed and a treatment plan designed, he took personal charge of his rehabilitation program. He initiated a recovery program that included an increase in salt and fluid intake and physical conditioning. He also worked hard at reducing the stress in his life and obtaining adequate hours of restful sleep.

Once diagnosed, Brandon jumped right in on his recovery program starting with:

- *Added exercising on a recumbent bicycle for 10 minutes daily to start, then 20 minutes, then 30 minutes daily 3 days per week.*

- *Increased intake of fluids to 3-4 quarts of sports drinks daily (not energy drinks). He was never seen without a sports drink bottle in his hand.*

- *Increased intake of salt, salty foods and adding generous sprinkling of salt onto his foods.*

Within 10 months, Brandon's symptoms began to subside and at 18 months he was well on the way to recovery.

If possible, request or purchase two sets of textbooks for your student, one to keep at school and one to keep at home. Not only are many of today's books very heavy to carry around, but those students experiencing "brain fog" may not remember which books to bring home on a specific day.

Severe memory loss causes a very challenging problem for teachers as they evaluate your child's understanding of class material when assigning grades. Having POTS can compromise the student's ability to remember, comprehend and retrieve information. It can also impair the student's ability to use the process of deductive reasoning to reach a logical conclusion. Some suggested alternatives for teachers are to base grades on understanding and participation during the actual class. Many students with POTS will be fine in the moment. They may be able to have lively discussions in class, but will be unable to remember class material when they wake up the next day. So, it's important to evaluate their participation during classes. Studying for tests can also be challenging. Some teachers have students participate in a quick oral exam right after class to evaluate their understanding of the material presented.

Other modifications to testing can include take home tests, shortening a test, breaking a test into several sections or letting the student take the test over several periods of time. Laptops, tape recorders, calculators and other technology aids could be made available to the student. There are even pens with built-in digital recorders and computer programs that can turn the spoken word (dictation) into printed text, without ever having to type.

Math and science are particularly difficult because these classes build on material learned the day before. Reading can cause headaches and getting one's thoughts together for writing can be daunting. If possible, take classes such as art, music, photography and film which are good options for electives. One eleventh grader said that the task of writing felt like "trying to ride a unicycle across the ocean."

If returning to school is not a possibility, then home schooling may be their only option. Try to have teachers prioritize lesson plans and homework so that the amount of work isn't overwhelming. Also, see if a few students in the class would be willing to take turns coming over once or twice a week to go over classroom material. As much as possible, try to keep your child connected to what is going on socially at school. Also, even if your child isn't able to go to school every day, if they feel able to go to school for after school activities they used to participate in, this should be encouraged. It's very easy to get depressed when you feel isolated from your friends at school.

Have your teen utilize post-it-notes, a small journal and/or their cell phone and laptop to record events that have happened and set alarms for upcoming activities. One mother used to write a note each night and put it on the floor by her child's bed. The note would include the day, date of the week and activities scheduled for that day. When their child awoke in the morning she/he would have no recollection of what day it was and what was happening. Her child also kept a memory journal where he would record events of the day or funny stories that happened with friends so he could keep up socially with his peers.

Standardized Testing Issues

Standardized testing is challenging as well. Talk to your student's college counselor well before tests so that your child can apply for accommodations for taking the SAT, ACT, AP and other tests. Some accommodations that are available are allowing for extra time and the ability to take the test over several sittings instead of all at one time.

Social Life - Importance of Friends

Being home in bed during the day can be extremely isolating and frustrating for a teen. It feels like everyone else's life is moving forward except theirs. POTS kids often feel that their life is either stopped or is moving backwards. With social media as a fundamental aspect of teen life, your child can see what everyone else is doing all day long. While everyone else is having fun and going to activities, events and parties, watching it on social media and not being able to participate is depressing. Understandably, try and get your child back into their social scene as quickly as possible. The best way to get connected back is through school and extracurricular activities.

If it's hard for your child to get out to parties and movies with friends, make sure your home is open to visiting friends. You should encourage your child to invite friends over to hang out. What the activity is, does not really matter. What's important is that they get to spend relaxing times with their friends. Most teens love coming over to watch their favorite movies. There are also lots of fun board, card and video games available that teens enjoy playing together. Just make sure there is a steady supply of pizza, popcorn, nachos, brownies, etc. If you make your house a comfortable place for your kid's friends to spend time, it will be easier to keep your child connected with their friends. However, sleepovers are not recommended because it is important that teens with POTS adhere to a regular sleep schedule and not stay up really late.

Mental Health Issues

Teens with POTS who have never had prior mental health challenges commonly become anxious or depressed. But to be clear, the POTS symptoms are not a result of anxiety or depression. The POTS illness comes first and the resultant anxiety and/or depression comes from loss of control over one's life due to the POTS symptoms. Suffering with a bizarre disruptive illness like POTS, can stress-out even the strongest among us.

For example, imagine being a popular athlete who went to every game and party, who now can't leave her room. One teen with POTS would go out to a movie with friends on Saturday night, only to call them up on Sunday to make plans with them to see the same movie again as she had no memory of seeing the movie the day before and thought it was still Saturday. Instances like this happen over and over to individuals with POTS. Some POTS patients may need to talk to a mental health specialist to deal with such very real frustrations.

Parents Tough Love Issues

Frequently, POTS patients spend months to years going from doctor to doctor and enduring test after test trying to figure out what's wrong. During that time, parents see their sick child's health continue to deteriorate, and they feel worse each month. Often, fatigue forces sick children to turn to homeschooling. Understandably, loving parents often become sympathetic, caring and coddling of their sick child. In addition to becoming caretakers, parents can often become strong advocates to fight for their child's diagnosis and dignity.

Initially, most patients are told many times that their symptoms are not real, "it's all in your head" or "you're making it up." However, once the POTS diagnosis is established, parents need to switch gears from viewing their child as "sick" to helping their child get better. Support must change from nurturing and coddling to a bit of tough love. The only person who can help your child feel better is your child. It is up to the POTS sufferer to make the lifestyle changes that will result in feeling better. POTS patients need to learn to be responsible for their own medication, salt and fluid intake, exercise and stress management strategies for their own recovery.

The world is lived vertically. It's important that POTS teens join the vertical world as soon as possible. That's the world they and their friends live in. They will need to fight through feeling awful and wanting to lie down and spend the day in bed. Even though it is very natural for a mom to say, "Oh honey, I know you feel bad. Just lie down and rest for a while until you feel better." This is not the best option, if you want your child to have as full a life as they can despite having POTS. Encouragement can include seeking opportunities to practice the Tips for Overcoming Venous Pooling and Tips for Healthy Breathing. Your child will need to become a fighter and you will need to provide tough encouragement to achieve **POWER over POTS.**

A General Guide to Parenting Behavioral Do's & Don'ts

Parents often exhibit behaviors that they think are helping their child, but they really aren't. Remaining neutral with respect to your child's pain is important Preferably, don't focus on the troubling behaviors your child may exhibit – such as complaining, listing what feels bad, lying down and refusing to get out of bed, etc. While of course you should be sympathetic to what they are experiencing, don't let them focus on describing their troubles in great detail. Instead, help them focus on their participation in their recovery strategies.

Behavioral Do's

- Do talk to your child about making a plan together for encouraging their participation in their recovery.

- Some kids want a gentle reminder from their parents to "use your strategies" while others don't. Do use distractions to keep your child focused on other more positive activities rather than their symptoms. A funny story, a silly joke, an art project, a sports game on TV, taking a short walk outside are all activities to redirect your child's focus away from their symptoms. Ask them what they would like to do and then do it. Also, encourage them to invite their friends over to hang out. Nothing is as good a distraction as friends visiting.

- Do encourage your child to use their strategies to cope with their symptoms. This book contains strategies for individuals with POTS. It lists behaviors they must do to help feel better. Unfortunately, behavioral change is never easy. Think about the last time you tried to change something in your life and how difficult it was for you. Now think about getting a discouraged teenager who doesn't feel well to change their behavior. Therefore, be supportive without being nagging. It is not the parent's job to remind their teens to drink fluids or do their exercise. Ultimately it is up to the teens themselves. But, positive support from you and encouragement is critical. If your child hasn't exercised in three days, but then does, saying something like "I know it must have been hard for you to work out today, but good for you for doing it." That is being supportive. Saying something like "You haven't exercised in three days, so don't complain to me about how bad you feel," is not helpful. Always be supportive and acknowledge progress and participation in the strategies, but refrain from commenting on a lack of adherence to the program. If your child is not actively doing what they are supposed to do to feel better and they complain to you about feeling badly, an appropriate response is "I'm sorry you aren't feeling well. Maybe you can try one of your strategies to feel better." Don't lecture your child or yell at them. Just stay calm and neutral and redirect them back to what they can control.

- Do be consistent. If there are two parents involved in raising the child, have a united front and be consistent. It is important for each parent to have the same limits and expectations for the child. While it is difficult for some parents to work together, it is in the best interest of your child if you can put your differences aside and be on the same page with respect to their POTS recovery. It will not be effective if one parent thinks the child should go back to school and the other parent thinks it's okay to spend the day home in bed. So, figure out how to work together.

- Do realize that some days will be harder for the child than others. Even without any extenuating circumstances, the nature of POTS is that symptoms can fluctuate from day to day. Add in school, activities and weekends, and it can be even more variable. So be supportive. If your child is having a bad day, don't regress back to old habits. Just help them get back on track by doing the steps they need to do.

- Do plan for special occasions. When you know there will be a change in their regular schedule such as trips, holidays, parties, etc. anticipate them and help your child plan for them by following their program methodically and consistently. The more they prepare for the event, the less the event will impact how they feel afterwards. Many POTS specialists report that a few days after parties and celebrations, they get an increase in phone calls from parents saying that their children, who were doing well, have now taken a turn for the worse. Going off a scheduled routine even for one night, can lead to a rough week ahead. It doesn't mean that kids with POTS can't participate in these special late night events; they just need to plan ahead for late night events. If they know that they will be up late for a special occasion, they need to get extra rest, fluids and salt in the days leading up to the event. They need to stick to a strict exercise plan and not miss a day even if they don't feel like it. How they feel after the special event is related to how they prepared for it the week before.

- Do praise them when they make entries in their fluid, salt and exercise Recovery Cards. Every entry is an important step towards taking charge of their health that will lead to POTS recovery and increased **POWER over POTS.**

Initially, most patients are told many times that their symptoms are not real, "it's all in your head" or "you're making it up." However, once the POTS diagnosis is established, parents need to switch gears from viewing their child as "sick" to helping their child get better.

Behavioral Don'ts

Don't ask your child how they are feeling. Constantly asking your child how they are feeling reinforces the "being sick" label.

Stop talking about POTS and all of the miserable symptoms that come with it. Asking how they feel, only reinforces the child focusing on their discomfort and symptoms. Your child has a plan and strategies to work through and minimize their symptoms (provided in this book). If they bring up feeling bad, your response should be to tell them to go use one of their strategies to feel better, not "go lie down."

Don't blame your child for feeling bad or complaining about their symptoms. You may be sick of hearing them talk about their symptoms, but it's better if you don't react. The best strategy again is to tell them that they have the tools to feel better and it's up to them to use them. Don't exempt them from house rules that should be followed, but have been forgiven because they are sick. If they have chores to do around the house, they should do them if they can. They might need to be modified, but they shouldn't be eliminated.

Don't make special exceptions for your child, if there are other children in the house following family rules. For example, if no cell phones are allowed at the table for other children, don't let your child with POTS break this rule simply because he or she has POTS. Sometimes you see sibling rivalry with the other siblings in the home. They may think that they have to follow rules while the "sick" kid can get away with anything because they have POTS. For example, the child with POTS may have to lie down after dinner and not help with the cleanup, but once everything has been cleaned up the child with POTS feels better and can walk around. Try and keep things consistent for all children and encourage the child with POTS to contribute to and follow the same rules as other members of the family.

Don't underestimate how some things you say to your child, while well meaning, can make things worse. Sometimes there are words or phrases parents use that make the child with POTS frustrated. Statements like "I know just how you feel" or "I understand what you are going through" can aggravate your child because the truth is, you don't. Have a conversation with your child and have them express what comments irritate them and make a plan for you to eliminate them from your conversation. I know of one family where the mom kept saying, "I understand how you feel" which made the kid furious. They agreed that every time she said it, she would put a $5.00 bill in a jar that the son would get to keep. They had a sense of humor about it and it helped her eliminate it from her speech pattern without increasing her child's frustration.

Travel Tips

Long rides or flights can be problematic as they discourage blood circulating up from the legs. Get up and walk around. Try and do leg exercises and refer to the Tips for Overcoming Venous Pooling.

Have a list of exercises that you can do both while sitting and standing in a plane. Wherever possible, fly direct without stop-overs thus shortening the travel day

Plan to be well hydrated before a plane trip because air travel promotes dehydration. Drink lots of water before your plane trip starting a few days before so that you start your trip well hydrated. Also bring water or a beverage with you on the plane. Sometimes if plane rides are bumpy, the flight attendants stop beverage service and they might not get to you. Therefore, make sure you bring plenty of drinks of your own.

Activities to Overcome Venous Pooling While Flying

Multiple opportunities are available each day to overcome venous pooling in the legs. The following activities strengthen the lower body muscular pumps and encourage venous return back to the heart. These exercises can be especially useful for prolonged sitting and flying.

Useful standing activities to consider

- Walk instead of standing still
- Contract (tighten) the abdominal, buttock (fanny), thigh and calf muscles repeatedly
- Shift weight from one leg to the other
- Stand on your toes and heels (rocking motion) alternately
- Stand on one leg and bend the other
- Stand on tiptoes as high as you can

Useful sitting activities to consider

- Raise and lower knees up toward chest
- Dance with your feet on the floor
- Roll ankles (draw circles with toes)
- Raise your toes and heels (rocking motion) alternately

- Cross legs together at the ankles and repeatedly squeeze legs together

- Cross legs together at the ankles and repeatedly raise legs

Avoid prolonged crossing legs when sitting as it impedes lower leg venous flow. And always, while exercising, keep breathing. Don't breath-hold while exercising.

Surgical Procedures

Surgical procedures present unique problems for individuals with POTS. The prohibited drinking of fluids pre-operatively does not go well with POTS patients as it worsens dehydration. Many teens with POTS experience worsening of POTS symptoms after surgeries even as minimal and routine as having wisdom teeth removed. Dentists especially, need to be aware that POTS patients do not tolerate sitting upright in a dental chair for a prolonged procedure. Therefore, before any surgical procedure, make sure your doctors (dentist, surgeon and anesthesiologist) are familiar with POTS and its management, particularly the need for avoiding upright positioning during the procedure and increased fluid intake both pre- and post-surgery.

Check with your doctors to see if your child can take their regular medications before and after surgery. Many doctors who treat POTS patients, recommend administering one or two extra bags (liters) of intravenous fluids after a surgical procedure. This is in addition to the intravenous fluids routinely given during surgery. Some times after surgery, POTS patients will have an increased pulse rate and decreased oxygen levels. These abnormalities may take a little longer to normalize when compared to individuals who don't have POTS. Also, if after surgery, your child is required to rest in bed for period of time, check with your child's doctor regarding their medications and fluid intake. Some doctors adjust medications during a period of non-active recuperation so as to minimize POTS symptoms until your child is able to get out of bed and resume walking.

Insurance Reimbursement

Whereas most medical personnel have little or no familiarity with POTS, it's understandable that medical insurance personnel have even less knowledge. Physicians caring for POTS patients, with all their complex issues, require considerable clinical experience and expertise. And of course, taking a meticulous history, performing a comprehensive physical examination and designing a personalized rehabilitation program take considerable time and skill. Unfortunately, medical insurance personnel don't appreciate the value of the medical skills and time required to improve the lives of POTS sufferers. And of course, generally they don't like paying reasonable fees for rendering care to POTS patients. Thus, often adding to the out-of-pocket costs experienced by caretakers of POTS patients.

Chapter 14 explains the **Prognosis for POTS Patients**

What Is the Prognosis for POTS Patients?

Under diagnoses and under treatment is unnecessary. Recovery is possible; unnecessary suffering can be remedied. Readjusting your physiology will not happen overnight. However, your status can now change for the better, **POWER over POTS is achievable!**

Each POTS patient has a unique combination of physiologic deviations from normal. Be it low blood volume, low salt intake, poor muscular strength and exercise intolerance, cardiac atrophy, inadequate sleep, stress or medications that aggravate POTS symptoms, Each patient's treatment needs to be individualized. Treatment needs to be tailored to correct those factors most important for each POTS patient and their own combination of correctable body changes. Therefore, it is important to seek the help of a POTS medical specialist to design a personalized **"Taking Back My Life"** program. Most alterations in body physiology responsible for reducing the return of blood from the lower body to the heart and brain are correctable with time and treatment. And remember, the first steps in behavioral change are always the hardest.

The prognosis is excellent for the majority of POTS patients. Most adolescents and adults with POTS will be greatly improved within 5 years. Based on the Mayo experience with over 500 POTS adolescent-onset patients, half reported persistent improved symptoms at 5 years. Nineteen percent reported complete clearance of symptoms and 16% reported only sporadic symptoms. Thus, investment in these behavioral changes and judicious use of medicine can return most POTS patients to normal fully active adult lives.

For the majority of POTS patients recovery is possible - unnecessary suffering can be remedied. No single treatment will be effective and readjusting one's physiology will not happen overnight. However, gradual significant improvement can be expected by following the recommended life-style adjustments of your POTS specialist and putting the behavioral changes provided in this book into action steps.

You need to constantly say to yourself the following:

I'm making every effort to get up and participate in upright activities as much as possible. Even when I find it difficult to do so, I'll push myself and I'll take back my life! **Success in Beating POTS is now in my hands**.

Only I can make this commitment to achieve **POWER over POTS**. I have no time for excuses! I want to take back my life! Only I can invest the time and effort in these behavioral changes and make possible my return to being a normal fully active adult.

Only I can take Action Steps to Recovery! Only I can establish and achieve goals for myself! Only I can celebrate my accomplishments! Only I can acquire POWER over POTS!

I'm Taking Back My Life

My To Do List – My Action Steps to Recovery

- Avoidance of Triggers
- Increase Fluid Intake
- Increase Salt Intake
- Increase Exercise
- Increase Upright Time
- Overcome Venous Pooling
- Increase Abdominal Breathing
- Improve Sleep
- Decrease Stress

Chapter 15 explains **POTS Terminology**

CHAPTER 15:

POTS Terminology

Acrocyanosis – Bluish-purple discoloration of skin of lower legs associated with venous pooling of blood in the legs.

Autonomic nervous system - The autonomic (automatic) nervous system is responsible for maintaining homeostasis (equilibrium) of the body's inner organs no matter the stressor. The autonomic nervous system controls all the body functions that work on auto-pilot like heartbeat, breathing, digestion, eye muscles and endocrine glands.

Baroreceptors – Pressure sensors within the major blood vessels that detect diminished blood flow and low blood pressure and stimulate the secretion of stress hormones.

Blood pressure – Pressure within arterial blood vessels as heart propels blood to circulate throughout the body

Carbon dioxide – Carbon dioxide is the byproduct of oxygen metabolism by bodily tissues. The carbon dioxide produced within tissues travels via the blood-stream to the lungs where it is exhaled. The body depends on this carbon dioxide travelling in the blood to combine with water and slightly acidify the blood.

Cardiac Output (CO) - Amount of blood ejected in cc per minute. Cardiac output equals SV (stroke volume) times HR (heart rate).

$$CO = SV \text{ times } HR$$

Cardiac output averages 16-32 cups/min among adolescents and adults. SV falls due to diminished cardiac filling in patients with POTS resulting in reduced CO. Sensors recognize this fall in CO, and the sympathetic nervous system shifts into overdrive, increasing heart rate in an attempt to raise CO and restore circulation to the vital organs.

Cerebral Blood Flow (CBF) – Blood circulating to the brain averages approximately 3 cups per minute. The brain depends on a stable and adequate flow of blood for oxygen, nourishment and maintenance of function. About 15% of the Cardiac Output supplies the brain with blood. The brain is very susceptible to hypoperfusion (diminished cerebral blood flow) and diminished blood flow results in ischemia (injury due to diminished cerebral blood flow). Among POTS patients, it is this ischemia that interferes with normal brain function and is responsible for the assortment of brain-related symptoms observed.

The prognosis is excellent for the majority of POTS patients. Most adolescents and adults with POTS will be greatly improved within 5 years. Based on the Mayo experience with over 500 POTS adolescent-onset patients, half reported persistent improved symptoms at 5 years.

Dysautonomia – A condition in which there is abnormal functioning of the autonomic nervous system (system that automatically controls most involuntary bodily functions). Nerves derived from the brain and spinal cord automatically (without voluntary input) carry messages that regulate the function of practically all organs of the body. When not working properly, this abnormal regulation of body function is referred to as dysfunction. Dysautonomia can be inherited or acquired. Autonomic dysfunction includes abnormalities of heart rate, blood pressure, blood flow, metabolism, breathing, swallowing, digestion, vision, sweating, tearing and genital function.

Only I can make this commitment to achieve POWER over POTS. I have no time for excuses! I want to take back my life! Only I can invest the time and effort in these behavioral changes and make possible my return to being a normal fully active adult.

POTS is a member of the dysautonomias that rarely includes postural hypotension with syncope (fainting). Most additional examples of dysautonomia may include postural hypotension with syncope (fainting). Fainting, dizziness and blurred vision can occur at the onset of standing or after prolonged sitting or standing. Examples of dysautonomia include mast cell activation disorder, diabetes mellitus, Parkinson's disease, autonomic failure, multi-system atrophy, familial dysautonomia, neurocardiogenic syncope, drugs and toxins.

Heart Rate [HR] – Heart beats per minute.

Head-up Tilt Test [HUTT] – Measurement of pulse and blood pressure while being tilted upright.

Hypertension – Elevated pressure within the blood vessels

Hyperventilation – Rapid rate of breathing

Hypotension - Diminished pressure within the blood vessels during acute blood loss, dehydration or medications

Hypovolemia – Diminished circulating blood volume

Norepinepherine – The stress hormone of the sympathetic nervous system

Orthostatic hypotension – A fall in blood pressure brought on by assuming the upright posture (>20 mmHg systolic and >10 mmHg diastolic). Generally associated with fainting or passing out due to serious medical conditions (not usually POTS).

Osmotic pressure – The ability of cell walls to control the flow of fluids from solutions of low to higher concentrations.

Palpitations – Awareness of an unusual rapid or irregular beating of the heart.

Physiological processes - Physiological processes describe the many body processes that maintain life, all mental and physical functions.

Pulmonary circulation – Portion of circulatory system that carries unoxygenated blood from the right heart to the lungs to pick-up oxygen and to exhale carbon dioxide and then returns the oxygenated blood to the left heart to circulate and nourish the entire body.

Renin-angiotensin aldosterone system - Volume sensors within the kidneys detect reduced blood volume and/or blood pressure and release renin to increase reabsorption of salt and water by the kidneys, increasing blood volume.

Signs – an outer body change that is observable by others such as bluish discoloration of the skin, passing out and trouble walking.

Stress hormones – Epinephrine (adrenalin) stimulates increased cardiac output, skeletal muscle blood flow, sodium retention, reduced intestinal motility, venous constriction, increased glucose release, widening of the bronchial tubes and preparation for battle.

Stroke Volume (SV) – Amount of blood ejected with each beat measured in cc (or ml) per beat. In adolescents SV averages 50-85 cc/beat and in adults averages 60-130 cc/beat. This amounts to about 2-2.5 ounces/beat in adolescents and 2-4 ounces/beat in adults. Hearts of females are generally smaller. Therefore, the SV in females tends to be a little lower.

Syncope – Fainting, passing out and/or loss of consciousness.

Symptoms – personal awareness of a bodily change such as fatigue, pain and dizziness.

Tachycardia – Rapid heart rate (normal heart rate is 60-100 beats per minute).

Tilt Table Test (TTT) - Measurement of pulse and blood pressure when standing upright compared to that obtained while lying flat.

Trans-Cranial Doppler – Research instrument utilized to non-invasively measure changes in cerebral perfusion (blood flow) within a major brain blood vessel.

Vaso-vagal syncope – Transient loss of vascular tone with abrupt fall in blood pressure and loss of consciousness due to cerebral hypoperfusion. Generally follows emotional stress, pain or medical procedures.

Venous flow - Flow of blood via veins back to the heart. Within the veins, the pressure is very low and the flow is likewise slow.

Venous return (VR) – Flow of blood via veins back to the heart. Muscular pumping of blood up from one venous valve to the next is responsible for accomplishing this difficult task against gravity. Cardiac output depends on adequate VR. However, among POTS patients venous return is reduced and so is cardiac output.

Chapter 16 provides your **POTS Resource Guide**.

CHAPTER 16:

POTS Resource Guide

Where to Find Help

Finding knowledgeable physicians and medical centers that specialize in diagnosing and treating patients with POTS is not easy. The most knowledgeable medical specialists are those that study patients with POTS. These include a limited number of cardiologists, pediatricians and neurologists. However, initial complaints frequently take patients to pediatricians, infectious disease specialists, internists, neurologists and family physicians - unfamiliar with POTS. Many of these physicians are not fully cognizant of POTS and its many bizarre presentations.

Few community physicians have access to the specialized testing described above and specialize in the recognition and management of POTS patients. For individuals with symptoms suggestive of POTS, it is important to seek a POTS knowledgeable professional to establish the correct diagnosis and then help customize an individualized optimal treatment program.

Medical Centers Specializing in POTS

Only a limited number of physicians primarily at specialized major medical centers have performed research on patients and have expertise with treating POTS. They may be cardiologists, neurologists, rheumatologists, gastroenterologists, pediatricians, exercise physiologists, psychiatrists, geneticists and behavioral health professionals. Finding these physicians who specialize in the treatment of POTS patients is often difficult. Centers with access to the specialized testing needed are best able to diagnose and manage POTS patients. For individuals with symptoms suggestive of POTS, it is important to seek a POTS knowledgeable professional to establish the correct diagnosis and then help customize an individualized treatment program

The following is a listing of some leading Medical Centers that have investigated POTS and published results of studies dealing with POTS. Apologetically, the names of specialists and phone numbers have been omitted because the staffing at these centers change frequently. Investigators regularly move from one medical center to another.

USA

Arizona

Mayo Clinic

Phoenix, Arizona

http://www.mayoclinic.org/patient-visitor-guide/arizona/
becoming-a-patient

Phoenix Children's Hospital, University of Arizona School of Medicine

Phoenix, Arizona

http://www.phoenixchildrens.com

California

Stanford University School of Medicine

Stanford, California

http://med.stanford.edu/neurology/divisions/autonomic.html

District of Columbia

Children's National Medical Center

Washington, District of Columbia

http://childrensnational.org

Illinois

University of Illinois at Chicago, Departments of Pediatrics & Medicine

Chicago, Illinois

www.hospital.uillinois.edu/primary-and-specialty-care/pediatrics/
childrens-hospital

Children's Hospital of Chicago, Center for Autonomic Medicine in Pediatrics

www.luriechildrens.org/en-us/care-services/specialties-services/center-for-autonomic-medicine/Pages/index.aspx

Iowa

University of Iowa Hospitals

Iowa City, Iowa

https://uichildrens.org/

Maryland

Johns Hopkins University, Department of Behavioral Biology

Baltimore, MD

www.hopkinsmedicine.org/medicine

National Institute of Neurological Disorders and Stroke

Bethesda, Maryland

www.ninds.nih.gov/about_ninds/addresses.htm

University of Maryland Medical Center, Department of Medicine

Baltimore, MD

www.umm.edu/programs/childrens/services/general-pediatrics

Massachusetts

Beth Israel Deaconess Medical Center, Autonomic and Peripheral Nerve Laboratory

Boston, MA

www.bidmc.org/Centers-and-Departments/Departments/Neurology/Autonomic-and-Peripheral-Nerve-Disorders.aspx

Boston University School of Medicine

Boston, MA

www.bumc.bu.edu/busm/about/contact-us/

Brigham and Women's Hospital, Department of Medicine

Boston, MA

www.brighamandwomens.org/Departments_and_Services/medicine/
default.aspx

Harvard Medical School, Department of Medicine

Boston, MA

www.hms.harvard.edu/contact-us

Michigan

Michigan Cardiovascular Institute, Central Michigan University

Saginaw, Michigan

http://www.cvi-mi.com

Minnesota

Mayo Clinic, Department of Pediatric and Adolescent Medicine

Rochester, MN

www.mayo.edu/research/department-divisions/department-neurology/
programs/division-child-adolescent-neurology

Mayo Clinic, Department of Autonomic Disorders

Rochester, MN

www.mayo.edu/research/department-divisions/department-neurology/
programs/ autonomic-nerve-disorders

New York

Columbia University Medical Center, Division Pediatric Neurology
New York, NY
www.columbianeurology.org/patient-care/child-neurology

New York Medical College, Department of Physiology and Pediatrics
Valhalla, NY
www.nymc.edu/.../fhp/centers/.../syncope/pots%20contacts/html

New York Presbyterian Hospital – Cornell Campus, Hypertension Division
New York, NY
www.nyp.org/services/neurology/html

SUNY Health Science Center, Department of Pediatrics
Syracuse, New York
www.upstate.edu/research/

Ohio

Cleveland Clinic Foundation, Department of Neurology
Cleveland, Ohio
www.my.clevelandclinic.org/services/heart/patient- education/webcharts/
autonomic-disorders

Nationwide Children's Hospital, Division of Pediatric Neurology
Columbus, Ohio
www.medicine.osu.edu/students/life/career-advising/specialists/pages/
childneurology.aspx

University of Toledo Medical Center, Syncope and Autonomic Disorders Center
Toledo, Ohio
www.uhealth.utoledo.edu/clinics/neurology

University Hospitals Case Medical Center, Department of Pediatrics

Cleveland, Ohio

www.uhospitals.org/general-pediatrics-and-adolescent-medicine

Pennsylvania

Children's Hospital of Philadelphia

Philadelphia, PA

www.chop.edu/conditions-diseases/

postural-orthostatic-tachycardia-syndrome-pots

Tennessee

Vanderbilt University, Autonomic Dysfunction Center

Nashville, TN

www.mc.vanderbilt.edu/root/vumc.php?site=adc&doc=38847

http://www.mc.vanderbilt.edu/root/vumc.php?site=adc

Texas

Baylor College of Medicine, Department of Pediatrics

Houston, Texas

https://www.bcm.edu/healthcare/care-centers/neuromuscular/

clinics-labs/autonomic-function-testing-laboratory

Texas Children's Hospital, Pediatric Clinic for Autonomic Dysfunction

Houston, Texas

http://www.texaschildrens.org/

find-a-department?name_1=pots+syndrome&=Search

**Texas Health Presbyterian Hospital, Institute Exercise &
Environmental Medicine**

Dallas, Texas

https://med.uth.edu/pediatrics/divisions/neurology/
sub-specialty-programs/dysautonomia-center-of-excellence

University of Texas Southwestern Medical Center
http://www.utsouthwestern.edu/education/medical-school/departments/
pediatrics/divisions/neurology/index.html

University of Texas, Pediatric Dysautonomia Center of Excellence
Houston, Texas
https://med.uth.edu/pediatrics/divisions/neurology/
sub-specialty-programs/dysautonomia-center-of-excellence/

Virginia
Children's Heart Institute
Reston, Virginia
www.chiva.com

Medical College of Virginia, Department of Medicine & Physiology
Richmond, Virginia
www.chrichmond.org/search.aspx?q=dysautonomia

West Virginia
West Virginia University, Department of Medicine
Morgantown, West Virginia
http://medicine.hsc.wvu.edu/pediatrics/

Wisconsin
Medical College of Wisconsin, Center for Pediatric Autonomic Disorders
Milwaukee, Wisconsin
www.cvrc.wisc.edu

World-Wide

Australia

Center for Heart Rhythm Disorders, University of Adelaide, Dept Cardiology
Royal Adelaide Hospital
South Australian Health and Medical Research Institute
Adelaide, Australia
www.adelaide.edu.au/chrd/people/

Baker Heart Research Institute, Human Neurotransmitter Laboratory
Melbourne, Victoria, Australia
www.abc.net.au/radionational/programs/healthreport/
research-at-the-baker-heart-research-institute-in/3428188

Charles Sturt University, School of Biomedical Sciences
Wagga Wagga, Australia
www.science.csu.edu.au/schools/biomed/staff

Royal Brisbane and Women's Hospital, Department of Neurology
Brisbane, Queensland, Australia
www.health.qld.gov.au/rbwh/services/neurology.asp

Brazil

Heart Institute – University of Sao Paulo Medical School
Sao Paulo, Brazil
www.fm.usp.br/site/Heart-Institute-InCor

British Columbia

University of British Columbia, Division of Cardiology
Vancouver, Canada

www.pediatrics.med.ubc.ca/divisions-centres/cardiology

Canada

Calgary University, Libin Cardiovascular Institute of Alberta Cumming School of Medicine
Calgary, Canada
www.libin.ucalgary.ca

Magill University, Autonomic Reflex Laboratory, Department of Neurology
Montreal, Quebec, Canada
www.mcgill.ca/research

University of Alberta, Department of Medicine, Division of Cardiology
Alberta, Canada
www.ualberta.ca/pediatrics/divisions/cardiology

University Hospital, London Health Sciences Center
Ontario, Canada
www.lhsc.on.ca/About_Us/LHSC/Contact_Us/index.htm

China

Peking University First Hospital, Department of Pediatrics
Beijing, China
www.manuscriptpro.com/profile/affiliation/Department-of-Pediatrics-Peking-University-First-Hospital-Beijing-China

England

National heart and Lung Institute, Imperial College
London, United Kingdom

https://www.imperial.ac.uk/nhli

Germany
University Hospital of Bonn, Institute of Human Genetics

Bonn, Germany

www.bookinghealth.com/university-hospital-bonn

Israel
Rambam Medical Center, Autonomic Dysfunction Center

Haifa, Israel

www.health-tourism.com/medical-centers/rambam-health-care-campus/
dep/neurology/

Italy
Oespedali del Tigullio

Lavagna, Italy

www.tigulliocardio.com

Japan
Shinshu University School of Medicine, Dept Sports Medical Sciences

Matsumoto, Japan

www.shinshu-u.ac.jp/faculty/medicine/eng/

United Kingdom
City Hospital, DGM Building

Birmingham, UK

www.swbh.nhs.uk/contact-locations/find-us/birmingham-city-hospital/

When All Else Fails

What about the adolescents and adults who don't make continuing improvement? What about the forty year old with unrecognized POTS for 20 years who doesn't make significant improvement? These patients may have a more severe form of POTS or one or more of the complex medical conditions that rarely accompany POTS. Many medical centers are available that focus on a variety of these rare complex medical co-conditions. Here, you find teams of specialists. It's no longer possible for a single specialist to know all there is to know concerning all the possible POTS combinations. You may need to discuss this with your primary care physician or specialist and request referral to one of the following super-specialists or centers where teams of physicians focus on a single aspect of POTS.

Dystonia Symptoms & POTS Specialists

Cardiologists	Best for:
	Tachycardia, palpitations, chest pain, shortness of breath, fatigue, blood pressure problems, exercise intolerance, standing intolerance, low energy
Gastroenterologists	Best for:
	Abdominal complaints weight loss, nausea, vomiting, abdominal pain, constipation, diarrhea, gastroparesis, bloating
Neurologists	Best for:
	Headaches, neck pain or numbness, upper arm pain or numbness, passing out, fatigue, weakness, visual disturbances, dizziness, forgetfulness, poor concentration, tremulousness, low energy, sleep disturbance, bladder disturbances
Geneticists	Best for:
	Familial dysautonomias, EDS, long fingers, double jointed arms and legs, increased flexibility, loose stretchy skin

Rheumatologist	Best for:
	Joint hypermobility, tissue fragility, unstable joints, joint pains, loose stretchy skin
Allergists/Immunologists	**Best for:**
	Episodic attacks, flushing, itching, hives, high blood pressure, low blood pressure, post-attack exhaustion,
Endocrinologists	**Best for:**
	Persistent tachycardia, nervousness, persistent sweating, anxiety, weight problems
Neurosurgeons	**Best for:**
	Episodic flushing, upper arm tingling, numbness or pain, loss bladder and colon control, difficulty swallowing, difficulty speaking
Gynecologists	**Best for:**
	Menstrual-related worsening of symptoms, pregnancy-related worsening of symptoms

Organizations Devoted to the POTS and Dysautonomia Information

POTS Syndrome blog

www.poweroverpots.com

American Academy of Neurology

www.aan.org

American Autonomic Society

www.americanautonomicsociety.org

Dysautonomia Foundation
www.familialdysautonomia.org

Dysautonomia Information Network
www.dinet.org

Dysautonomia Youth Network of America, Inc.
www.dynainc.org

Ehlers-Danlos National Foundation
www.ednf.org

Mayo Clinic
www.mayo.edu/research/departments-divisions/department-neurology/programs/autonomic-nerve-disorders

National Dysautonomia Research Foundation
www.ndrf.org

National Institutes of Neurological Disorders & Strokes (NINDS)
www.ninds.nih.gov

National Organization for Rare Disorders (NORD)
www.rarediseases.org

Postural Tachycardia Syndrome
www.ninds.nih.gov/disorders/postural_tachycardia_syndrome/postural_tachycardia_syndrome.htm

Postural Tachycardia Syndrome - Circulation
www.circ.ahajournals.org/content/117/21/2814.full

Postural Tachycardia Syndrome - Circulation

www.circ.ahajournals.org/content/127/23/2336.full

PUBMED

www.pubmed.com

Rare Disease Network

www.rarediseasenetwork.org

Finding Clinical Studies Dealing with POTS

www.clinicaltrials.gov

This Clinical Trials web-site (a service of the U.S. National Institutes of Health) provides a brief overview of clinical research, information for potential clinical study participants, and a glossary of common words used on ClinicalTrials.gov. It provides information on eligibility to participate in a study, questions to ask when considering whether to participate in a study and what happens during a study.

POTS related clinical trials world-wide are listed here. While the majority of research studies (45/60 at the time of publication) are available in the U.S., it's important to recognize the world-wide interest in POTS research. Twenty-four were actively recruiting patients. Many of the trials offer opportunities to contribute to the evolving scientific knowledge dealing with the mechanisms and potential treatments for patients with POTS.

Recommended Publications

Postural tachycardia syndrome

Arnold, A.C., Hama, K., et al. Cognitive dysfunction in postural tachycardia syndrome. *Clinical Science.* 2015;128:39-45

Benarroch, E. E. Postural tachycardia syndrome: a heterogeneous and multifactorial disorder. *Mayo Clinic Proceedings.*2012;87(12)1214-1225

Bhatia, R., Kizilbash, S.J., et al. Outcomes of adolescent-onset postural orthostatic tachycardia syndrome. *Journal of Pediatrics.*2016;173:149-153

Brianna, L., Haeri, S. A case report and review of postural orthostatic tachycardia syndrome in pregnancy. *American Journal Perinatology Reports.*2015;5:e33-e36

Freeman, R., Wieling, W. Consensus statement on the definition of orthostatic hypotension, neutrally mediated syncope and the postural tachycardia syndrome. *Clinical Autonomic Research.*2011;21:69-72

Fried, R. The breath connection. *Insight Books.*1990

Fu, Q., Levine, B.D. Exercise in the postural tachycardia syndrome. *Autonomic Neuroscience: Basic and Clinical.2015;188:86-89*

Fu, Q., VanGundy, T. B., et al. Cardiac origins of the postural orthostatic tachycardia syndrome. *Journal of the American College of Cardiology Foundation.*2010;55(25):2858-2868

Fu, Q., VanGundy, T. B., et al. Menstrual cycle affects renal-adrenal and hemodynamic responses during prolonged standing in the postural orthostatic tachycardia syndrome. *Hypertension.*2010;56(1):82-90

Garland, E.M., Caledonio, J.E., et al. Postural Tachycardia Syndrome: Beyond Orthostatic Intolerance. *Current Neurology Neuroscience Report.2015;22:1-11*

Heyer, L. H., Fedak, E. M. Symptoms predictive of postural tachycardia syndrome (POTS) in the adolescent headache patient. *Headache.* 2013;53:947-953

Huang, H., Deb, A., et al. Dermatological manifestations of postural tachycardia syndrome are common and diverse. *Journal Clinical Neurology.2016;12(1):75-78*

Huang, R. J., Chun, C. L., et al. Manometic abnormalities in the postural orthostatic tachycardia syndrome: a case series. *Digestive Diseases Science.2013;58:3207-3211*

Jacob, G., Costa, F., et al. The neuropathic postural tachycardia syndrome. *The New England Journal of Medicine.* 2000;343(14):1008-1014

Jarjour, I. T. Postural tachycardia syndrome in children and adolescents. *Seminars in Pediatric Neurology.* 2013;20:18-26

Johnson, J.N., Mack, K. J., et al. Postural orthostatic tachycardia syndrome: a clinical review. *Pediatric Neurology.2009;42:77-85*

Kimpiski, K., Iodice, V., et al. Effect of pregnancy on postural tachycardia syndrome. *Mayo Clinic Proceedings.* 2010;85(7):639-644

Kizilbash, S. J., Ahrens, S. P., et al. Adolescent fatigue, POTS and recovery: a guide for clinicians. *Current Problems Pediatric Adolescent Health Care.* 2014;44:108-133

Lambert, E., Lambert, G. W. Sympathetic dysfunction in vasovagal syncope and the postural orthostatic tachycardia syndrome. *Frontiers in Physiology.* 2014;5:1-9

Loavenbruck, A., Turrino, J. et al. Disturbances of gastrointestinal transit and autonomic functions in postural orthostatic tachycardia syndrome. *Gastroenterology & Motility.* 2014;27

Low, Phillip A., Sandroni, Paola. Postural tachycardia syndrome (POTS). *Journal of Cardiovascular Electrophysiology.*2009;20(3):352-358

Mack, K. J., Johnson, J.N., et al. Orthostatic intolerance and the headache patient. *Seminars in Pediatric Neurology:*2010;17:109-116

Medow, M.S., Postural tachycardia syndrome from a pediatric perspective. *The Journal of Pediatrics.* 2011;158(1):5-7

Moon, J., Lee, H.S., et al. The complexity of diagnosing postural tachycardia syndrome: influence of the diurnal variability. *Journal of the American Society of Hypertension.* 2016;10(3):263-270

Ocon, A. J., Medow, M.S., et al. Decreased upright cerebral blood flow and cerebral autoregulation in normocapnic postural tachycardia syndrome. *American Journal Physiological Society.* 2009;29(2):664-673

Pollack, A.A., Wood E.H. Venous pressure in the saphenous vein at the ankle in man during exercise and changes in posture. *Journal of Applied Physiology.*1948;1:649-662

Rabbitts, J. A., Groenewald, C. B., et al. Postural orthostatic tachycardia syndrome and general anesthesia: a series of 13 cases. *Journal of Clinical Anesthesia.*2011;23:384-392

Raj, S. R. Postural tachycardia Syndrome (POTS). *Circulation.* 2013;127:2336 2342

Ross, A.J., Ocon, A.J., et al. A double-blind placebo-controlled crossover study of the vascular effects of midodrine in neuropathic compared with Hyperadrenergic postural tachycardia syndrome. *Clinical Science.* 2014;126(4):289-296

Safder, S., Chelimsky, T. C., et al. Autonomic testing in functional gastrointestinal disorders: implications of reproducible gastrointestinal complaints during tilt table testing. *Gastroenterology Research and Practice.*2009; Article ID 868496:1-6

Sheldon, R.S., Grubb, B.P., et al. 2015 Heart rhythm society expert consensus statement on diagnosis and treatment of postural tachycardia syndrome, inappropriate sinus tachycardia, and vasovagal syncope. *Heart Rhythm.*2015;12(6):42-57

Stewart, J. M., Common syndromes of orthostatic intolerance. Pediatrics.2013;131:968-980

Stewart, J. M., Medow, M.S., et al. Splanchnic hyperemia and hypervolemia during Valsalva maneuver in postural tachycardia syndrome. *American Journal Physiology of Heart Circulation Physiology.* 2005;289(5):H1951-H1959

Stewart, J. M., Medow, M.S., et al. Postural hypocapnic hyperventilation is associated with enhanced peripheral vasoconstriction in postural tachycardia syndrome with normal supine blood flow. *American Journal Physiology of Heart Circulation Physiology.* 2006;291(2):H904-H913

Stewart, J.M., Weldon, A. The relation between lower limb pooling and blood flow during orthostasis in the postural orthostatic tachycardia syndrome of adolescents. *Journal of Pediatrics.*2001;138:512-9

Tani, H., Singer, W., et al. Splanchnic-mesenteric capacitance bed in the postural tachycardia syndrome (POTS). *Autonomic Neuroscience: Basic and Clinical.*2000;86:107-113

Thieben, M. J., Sandroni, P. Postural orthostatic tachycardia syndrome: the mayo clinic experience. *Mayo Clinic Proceedings.* 2007;82(3):308-313

Wang, L.B., Culbertson, C.J., et al. Gastrointestinal dysfunction in postural tachycardia syndrome. *Journal of Neurological Sciences.*2015;359(1-2):193-196

Ehlers-Danlos syndrome

Grigoriou, E., Boris, J. R., et al. Postural orthostatic tachycardia syndrome (POTS): Association with Ehlers-Danlos syndrome and orthopedic considerations: *Clinical Orthopedics and Related Research.*2015;473:722-728

Kovacic, K., Cheliminsky, T.C., et al. Joint hypermobility: a common association with complex functional gastrointestinal disorders. *Journal Pediatrics.*2014;165:973-8

Wallman, D., Weinberg, J., et al. Ehlers-Danlos syndrome and postural tachycardia syndrome: a relationship study. *Journal of Neurological Sciences.*2014;340:99-102

Mast cell activation syndrome

Afrin, L.B., The presentation, diagnosis and treatment of mast cell activation syndrome. *Current Allergy & Clinical Immunology.*2014;27(3):146-150

Afrin, L.B., Never Bet Against Occam: Mast cell activation disease and the modern epidemics of chronic illness and medical complexity. *SistersMedia.*2016

Ain, C., Valent, P., et al. Mast cell activation syndrome: Proposed diagnostic criteria. *J Allergy Clinical Immunology*. 2010;126:1099-1104

Frieri, M., Oatel, R.,et al. Mast cell activation syndrome: a review. *Journal Current Allergy and Asthma Reports.*2013;13:27-32f mast cell activation

Hamilton, M., Hornick, J. et al. Mast cell activation syndrome: a newly recognized disorder with systemic clinical manifestations. *Journal Allergy and Clinical Immunology.*2011;128(1):147-152

Molderings, G. J., Brettner, S., et al. Mast cell activation disease: a concise practical guide for diagnostic workup and therapeutic options. *Journal of Hematology & Oncology.*2011;4:10

Soderberg, M. L. The mast cell activation syndrome: a mini review. *MOJ Immunology.*2015;2(1):1-4

Median arcuate ligament syndrome

Al-Bayati, I., McCallum, R.W. Median arcuate ligament syndrome. *Practical Gastroenterolgy.*2015;39(2):20-25

Horton, K.M., Talamini, M.A. et al. Median arcuate ligament syndrome: evaluation with CT angiography. *Radiographics.*2005;25:1177-1182

Kim, E., Lamb, K., et al. Median arcuate ligament syndrome-review of this rare disease. *JAMA Surgery.*2016;151(5):471-7

CHAPTER 17:

My POTS Recovery Cards

My POTS Recovery Cards
for INCREASING FLUID INTAKE

I KNOW HOW TO MANAGE POTS
INCREASING FLUID INTAKE IS IMPORTANT FOR ME

	M	T	W	T	F	S	S
AM							
LUNCH							
PM							
DINNER							
EVENING							
TOTALS							

GOAL

DAILY/WEEKLY

TOTAL

INCREASED FLUID INTAKE
IS KEY TO FEELING BETTER

My POTS Recovery Cards
for INCREASING FLUID INTAKE

I KNOW HOW TO MANAGE POTS
INCREASING FLUID INTAKE IS IMPORTANT FOR ME

	M	T	W	T	F	S	S
AM							
LUNCH							
PM							
DINNER							
EVENING							
TOTALS							

GOAL

DAILY/WEEKLY

TOTAL

INCREASED FLUID INTAKE
IS KEY TO FEELING BETTER

My POTS Recovery Cards
for INCREASING FLUID INTAKE

I KNOW HOW TO MANAGE POTS
INCREASING FLUID INTAKE IS IMPORTANT FOR ME

	M	T	W	T	F	S	S
AM							
LUNCH							
PM							
DINNER							
EVENING							
TOTALS							

GOAL

DAILY/WEEKLY

TOTAL

INCREASED FLUID INTAKE
IS KEY TO FEELING BETTER

My POTS Recovery Cards
for INCREASING FLUID INTAKE

I KNOW HOW TO MANAGE POTS
INCREASING FLUID INTAKE IS IMPORTANT FOR ME

	M	T	W	T	F	S	S
AM							
LUNCH							
PM							
DINNER							
EVENING							
TOTALS							

GOAL

DAILY/WEEKLY

TOTAL

INCREASED FLUID INTAKE
IS KEY TO FEELING BETTER

My POTS Recovery Cards
for INCREASING Salt INTAKE

Selecting Foods High in Sodium
Each numbered circle = 100s of mgs of Sodium [approximates]

restaurant dinners	⑱	deli pastrami, turkey	⑥
cured, smoked meats and fish	⑮	tomato juice, vegetable cocktail (1 cup)	⑥
potato salad (1 cup)	⑬	spaghetti sauce (½ cup), mashed potato (1 cup)	⑥
salt (1/2 tsp)	⑫	luncheon meats (2 slices), hamburger (1)	⑤
frozen dinners	⑪	pizza, cheese meat topping (1 slice)	④
broths, soups, baked beans and chili (1 cup)	⑩	tomato based sauces (1/4 cup)	④
potato au gratin	⑩	Italian sauce (1/2 cup),	④
soy sauce (1 Tbs)	⑨	canned vegetables (1/2 cup)	④
tuna salad (1 cup), sandwich burger (1)	⑧	pepperoni, salami (5 slices), bacon (3 slices)	④
cheese-burger, grilled chicken sandwich (1)	⑧	cheese (2 slices), cottage cheese (1/2 cup)	④
canned soups (1 can)	⑧	biscuit, bagel, croissant (1), pancake(2)	④
dill pickle (1), pretzels hard salted (10)	⑧	chili and cocktail sauce (2 Tbs)	④
instant noodle soup (packet)	⑧	apple, cherry pie (1 slice)	③
hot dog, smoked sausage, ham slice	⑦	salad dressings (2 Tbs)	③

I KNOW HOW TO MANAGE POTS
INCREASING SALT INTAKE IS IMPORTANT FOR ME

Daily Salt Tracker [Month] _____ [Day] _____

AM	
LUNCH	
PM	
DINNER	
EVENING	
TOTALS	

① ② ③ ④ ⑤ ⑥ ⑦ ⑧ ⑨ ⑩ ⑪ ⑫ ⑬ ⑭ ⑮ ⑯ ⑰ ⑱ ⑲ ⑳

Goal

Daily

TOTAL

INCREASED SODIUM INTAKE IS
KEY TO FEELING BETTER

My POTS Recovery Cards
for INCREASING Salt INTAKE

Selecting Foods High in Sodium
Each numbered circle = 100s of mgs of Sodium [approximates]

restaurant dinners	(18)	deli pastrami, turkey	(6)
cured, smoked meats and fish	(15)	tomato juice, vegetable cocktail (1 cup)	(6)
potato salad (1 cup)	(13)	spaghetti sauce (½ cup), mashed potato (1 cup)	(6)
salt (1/2 tsp)	(12)	luncheon meats (2 slices), hamburger (1)	(5)
frozen dinners	(11)	pizza, cheese meat topping (1 slice)	(4)
broths, soups, baked beans and chili (1 cup)	(10)	tomato based sauces (1/4 cup)	(4)
potato au gratin	(10)	Italian sauce (1/2 cup),	(4)
soy sauce (1 Tbs)	(9)	canned vegetables (1/2 cup)	(4)
tuna salad (1 cup), sandwich burger (1)	(8)	pepperoni, salami (5 slices), bacon (3 slices)	(4)
cheese-burger, grilled chicken sandwich (1)	(8)	cheese (2 slices), cottage cheese (1/2 cup)	(4)
canned soups (1 can)	(8)	biscuit, bagel, croissant (1), pancake(2)	(4)
dill pickle (1), pretzels hard salted (10)	(8)	chili and cocktail sauce (2 Tbs)	(4)
instant noodle soup (packet)	(8)	apple, cherry pie (1 slice)	(3)
hot dog, smoked sausage, ham slice	(7)	salad dressings (2 Tbs)	(3)

I KNOW HOW TO MANAGE POTS
INCREASING SALT INTAKE IS IMPORTANT FOR ME

Daily Salt Tracker [Month] _____ [Day] _____

AM	
LUNCH	
PM	
DINNER	
EVENING	
TOTALS	

(1)(2)(3)(4)(5)(6)(7)(8)(9)(10)(11)(12)(13)(14)(15)(16)(17)(18)(19)(20)

Goal

DAILY

TOTAL

INCREASED SODIUM INTAKE IS
KEY TO FEELING BETTER

My POTS Recovery Cards
for INCREASING Salt INTAKE

Selecting Foods High in Sodium
Each numbered circle = 100s of mgs of Sodium [approximates]

restaurant dinners	(18)	deli pastrami, turkey	(6)
cured, smoked meats and fish	(15)	tomato juice, vegetable cocktail (1 cup)	(6)
potato salad (1 cup)	(13)	spaghetti sauce (½ cup), mashed potato (1 cup)	(6)
salt (1/2 tsp)	(12)	luncheon meats (2 slices), hamburger (1)	(5)
frozen dinners	(11)	pizza, cheese meat topping (1 slice)	(4)
broths, soups, baked beans and chili (1 cup)	(10)	tomato based sauces (1/4 cup)	(4)
potato au gratin	(10)	Italian sauce (1/2 cup),	(4)
soy sauce (1 Tbs)	(9)	canned vegetables (1/2 cup)	(4)
tuna salad (1 cup), sandwich burger (1)	(8)	pepperoni, salami (5 slices), bacon (3 slices)	(4)
cheese-burger, grilled chicken sandwich (1)	(8)	cheese (2 slices), cottage cheese (1/2 cup)	(4)
canned soups (1 can)	(8)	biscuit, bagel, croissant (1), pancake(2)	(4)
dill pickle (1), pretzels hard salted (10)	(8)	chili and cocktail sauce (2 Tbs)	(4)
instant noodle soup (packet)	(8)	apple, cherry pie (1 slice)	(3)
hot dog, smoked sausage, ham slice	(7)	salad dressings (2 Tbs)	(3)

I KNOW HOW TO MANAGE POTS
INCREASING SALT INTAKE IS IMPORTANT FOR ME

Daily Salt Tracker [Month] _____ [Day] _____

AM	
LUNCH	
PM	
DINNER	
EVENING	
TOTALS	

(1)(2)(3)(4)(5)(6)(7)(8)(9)(10)(11)(12)(13)(14)(15)(16)(17)(18)(19)(20)

Goal

[   ]

DAILY

[   ]

TOTAL

INCREASED SODIUM INTAKE IS
KEY TO FEELING BETTER

My POTS Recovery Cards
for INCREASING Salt INTAKE

Selecting Foods High in Sodium
Each numbered circle = 100s of mgs of Sodium [approximates]

restaurant dinners	⑱	deli pastrami, turkey	⑥
cured, smoked meats and fish	⑮	tomato juice, vegetable cocktail (1 cup)	⑥
potato salad (1 cup)	⑬	spaghetti sauce (½ cup), mashed potato (1 cup)	⑥
salt (1/2 tsp)	⑫	luncheon meats (2 slices), hamburger (1)	⑤
frozen dinners	⑪	pizza, cheese meat topping (1 slice)	④
broths, soups, baked beans and chili (1 cup)	⑩	tomato based sauces (1/4 cup)	④
potato au gratin	⑩	Italian sauce (1/2 cup),	④
soy sauce (1 Tbs)	⑨	canned vegetables (1/2 cup)	④
tuna salad (1 cup), sandwich burger (1)	⑧	pepperoni, salami (5 slices), bacon (3 slices)	④
cheese-burger, grilled chicken sandwich (1)	⑧	cheese (2 slices), cottage cheese (1/2 cup)	④
canned soups (1 can)	⑧	biscuit, bagel, croissant (1), pancake(2)	④
dill pickle (1), pretzels hard salted (10)	⑧	chili and cocktail sauce (2 Tbs)	④
instant noodle soup (packet)	⑧	apple, cherry pie (1 slice)	③
hot dog, smoked sausage, ham slice	⑦	salad dressings (2 Tbs)	③

I KNOW HOW TO MANAGE POTS
INCREASING SALT INTAKE IS IMPORTANT FOR ME

Daily Salt Tracker [Month] _____ [Day] _____

AM	
LUNCH	
PM	
DINNER	
EVENING	
TOTALS	

①②③④⑤⑥⑦⑧⑨⑩⑪⑫⑬⑭⑮⑯⑰⑱⑲⑳

Goal

DAILY

TOTAL

INCREASED SODIUM INTAKE IS
KEY TO FEELING BETTER

My POTS Recovery Cards
for INCREASING Exercise

I KNOW HOW TO MANAGE POTS
INCREASING EXERCISE IS IMPORTANT FOR ME

	M	T	W	T	F	S	S
AM							
LUNCH							
PM							
DINNER							
EVENING							
TOTALS							

BECOMING MORE ACTIVE IS
THE BEST MEDICINE FOR ME

GOAL

WEEKLY

TOTAL

My POTS Recovery Cards
for INCREASING Exercise

I KNOW HOW TO MANAGE POTS
INCREASING EXERCISE IS IMPORTANT FOR ME

	M	T	W	T	F	S	S
AM							
LUNCH							
PM							
DINNER							
EVENING							
TOTALS							

BECOMING MORE ACTIVE IS
THE BEST MEDICINE FOR ME

GOAL

WEEKLY

TOTAL

My POTS Recovery Cards
for INCREASING Exercise

I KNOW HOW TO MANAGE POTS
INCREASING EXERCISE IS IMPORTANT FOR ME

	M	T	W	T	F	S	S
AM							
LUNCH							
PM							
DINNER							
EVENING							
TOTALS							

BECOMING MORE ACTIVE IS
THE BEST MEDICINE FOR ME

GOAL

WEEKLY

TOTAL

My POTS Recovery Cards
for INCREASING Exercise

I KNOW HOW TO MANAGE POTS
INCREASING EXERCISE IS IMPORTANT FOR ME

	M	T	W	T	F	S	S
AM							
LUNCH							
PM							
DINNER							
EVENING							
TOTALS							

BECOMING MORE ACTIVE IS
THE BEST MEDICINE FOR ME

GOAL

WEEKLY

TOTAL

Only I can take Action Steps to Recovery!
Only I can establish and achieve goals for myself!
Only I can celebrate my accomplishments!

Only I can acquire POWER over POTS!

Remember: Failing to Plan = Planning to Fail

I Can Take Charge!! Set Goals!!

I Too Can Recover!!

I Can Gain POWER over POTS!!

I'm Taking Back My Life